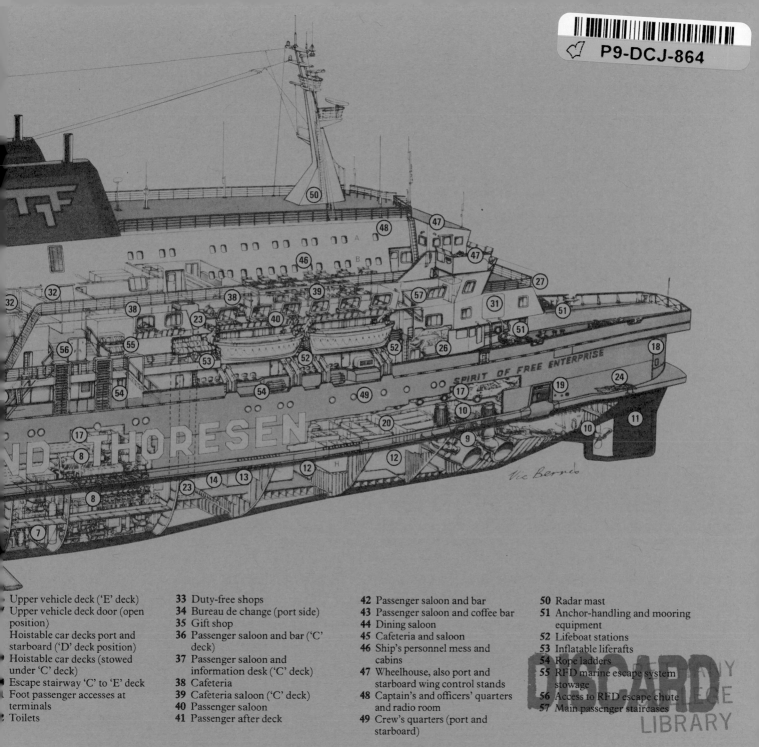

SPIRIT OF FREE ENTERPRISE

Vic Berris

(front cover) *Limatula*, a 320000-ton tanker, built in Denmark by Odense and belonging to Shell Tankers. Although not of the very largest size, this vessel is quite typical of the vast tank ships that carry the world's oil. Photo: Shell

(back cover) *Windsor Castle*, one of the finest of the last generation of true passenger liners. Photo: Union-Castle

ISBN 0 11 290320 7

Design by HMSO Graphic Design

Printed in England for
Her Majesty's Stationery Office
by Balding & Mansell, Wisbech, Cambs

Dd 696381   C150

AD FINEM FIDELIS

Hurl

National Maritime Museum

THE SHIP

The Revolution in Merchant Shipping

1950-1980

Ewan Corlett

London
Her Majesty's Stationery Office

Contents

Batillus, the world's largest ship in her building dock. Photo: Chantiers de l'Atlantique

Introduction by the General Editor

This is the last of a series of ten short books on the development of the ship, both the merchant vessel and the specialised vessel of war, from the earliest times to the present day, commissioned and produced jointly by the National Maritime Museum and Her Majesty's Stationery Office.

The books are each self-contained, each dealing with one aspect of the subject, but together they cover the evolution of vessels in terms which are detailed, accurate and up to date. They incorporate the latest available information and the latest thinking on the subject, but they are readily intelligible to the non-specialist, professional historian or layman.

Above all, as should be expected from the only large and comprehensive general historical museum in the world which deals especially with the impact of the sea on the development of human culture and civilisation, the approach is unromantic and realistic. Merchant ships were and are machines for carrying cargo profitably. They carried the trade and, in the words of the very distinguished author of the second book of the series, 'The creation of wealth through trade is at the root of political and military power.' The vessel of war, the maritime vehicle of that power, follows, and she is a machine for men to fight from or with.

It follows from such an approach that the illustrations to this series are for the most part from contemporary sources. The reader can form his own conclusions from the evidence, written and visual. We have not commissioned hypothetical reconstructions, the annotation of which, done properly, would take up much of the text.

This series began with Dr Sean McGrail's *Rafts, Boats and Ships*, an original and important contribution to the body of published work on the archaeology of water transport. It ends with new and original work in a totally different field, the industrial history of merchant shipping in the late 20th century.

As this series of books has shown, the study of the story of the ship begins with the scientific examination of the archaeological evidence, such as that provided by surviving ancient log boats. It goes on through the study of the evolution of the edge-joined, shell-built vessel, to the revolutionary and at present still mysterious development of the skeleton-built three-masted sailing ship in the 15th century. This very important vehicle slowly grew to be the relatively efficient wooden square-rigged sailing vessel of the early 19th century, and only one other important development took place, that of the schooner, essentially a product of the 18th century.

But in the early 19th century a great deal of essentially preparatory development work was done as a result of which, with the introduction of high pressure boilers of compound and triple expansion marine steam engines between 1865 and the early 1880s, a second great revolution in shipping took place and the normal merchant ship became the bulk-carrying steamer. Steel square-rigged sailing vessels and wooden multi-masted schooners, each type developed almost out of recognition and up to ten times the size of their predecessors, operated a number of long-range bulk trades until the First World War. Small sailing vessels survived until diminished by developments on land in the mid-20th century.

In the second half of the 20th century, merchant shipping has undergone as great and rapid a development as in the same period in the 15th century or the 19th. This third revolution is described in this book.

The story of the last of the three great periods of change is told by Dr Ewan Corlett, a leading practising naval architect whose strongly developed interest in the history of shipping had led him to play a major role in the salving and restoration of the historic steamship *Great Britain*, now on public display in Bristol.

Basil Greenhill

DIRECTOR, NATIONAL MARITIME MUSEUM

General Editor

United States, the fastest merchant ship ever built.
Photo: Skyfotos

The scope of the revolution

The rate of development of a technology is not unlike the flow of a great river—swift progress through rapids alternating with slow, steady progress in the open reaches between and, not infrequently, tributaries feeding in new flows. Generally, if not always, the rapids have been wars or their results bringing with them massive social changes, greatly increased motivation and expenditure on development and, finally, the inevitable need afterwards to develop new industries and markets. Tributary flows have come from the interaction with other and parallel technologies.

Not least has this applied to merchant shipping and ships. In the years between 1950 and 1980, a revolution has taken place, unprecedented except, perhaps, in Queen Victoria's reign. The technological aspects of the revolution were paralleled by the years between 1830 and 1860 and the immense development springing from this technological progress which took place between 1860 and 1890. In our era not only have the shapes and sizes of many ships altered out of all recognition but the whole pattern of world trade and of the carriage of goods by ships has changed more radically than in any comparable period in the history of shipping.

The start of the entire process was probably around the time Victoria became Queen, when the economies offered by increasing the size of ships became apparent to an enlightened few. Spurred by the need to carry the amount of coal required by the inefficient engines of the day, this pressure to increase size and the development of efficient multi-expansion engines led inevitably to iron, steel and steam overwhelming the wood- and wind-driven technologies of the day. The size of both steam- and wind-driven vessels increased rapidly at first, until a point was reached in the 1880s when the normal deep sea vessel was about the size of the 'monsters' of the 1840s, such as the *Great Britain*.

Except for passenger vessels on the Atlantic, where size meant speed and speed meant everything, and on long-range passenger routes such as to South Africa, the Far East and Australia, where size meant comfort and the ability to steam long distances without bunkering, vessels thereafter grew but slowly. So, by about 1880, a pattern was established which certainly lasted until the First World War and arguably for some time thereafter. Much progress was made but it was evolutionary rather than revolutionary. Labour and fuel costs were more or less static, a massive infra-structure of parts and estuaries and of small parcel cargo flows all militated against rapid increases in size and changes in the technology of carrying the world's goods.

The First World War began a change but it was slow. Oil started to replace coal, but by 1920 was still only supplying one tenth as much energy. This in itself was not a spur because the low price of coal was paralleled by that of the new oil, of which there was a surplus. After the war, the old Empires remained in being, their trading patterns unchanged. Ships did increase in size and design but only to a modest degree.

Passengers were carried in much the same ships as 30 or 40 years before, generally rather bigger, faster and more comfortable but similar in layout and performance. General cargo was carried break bulk by liners on established trade routes and by tramp ships all over the world. Cargo handling was in small parcels by derricks, or by cranes in the more developed ports. The cargo carriers of the world steamed generally between 9 and 14 knots. Oil tankers rarely exceeded 12 000 tons deadweight but their numbers did begin to increase quite rapidly with the spreading use of oil. Ports, too, were recognisably those of the last century, with congested access, cluttered storage and general reliance on a large labour force.

The Second World War, too, on the face of things, did not change methods much. Vast quantities of replacement tonnage were built, generally based upon pre-war designs, and when peacetime reconstruction commenced, most countries and shipping lines simply returned to the old patterns and built improved versions of pre-war vessels.

Nevertheless, appearances were deceptive and, in the event, the Second World War did change everything. Perhaps the changes arose from three or four main factors: the breakdown of established Empires and their trading systems leading to new ones, to new men and ideas in shipping; the massive development in methods of moving men and materials, above all for the invasion of Europe, where almost any idea that could work was tried; and, finally, the conception and development during the war of many of the basic tools needed for a revolution in technology and only waiting for commercial applications.

It is not often realised just how *avant-garde* were the methods used for the invasion of Europe: artificial harbours with spudded platforms; legs that could both anchor and elevate them when lowered to the sea bed; mobile pipelines; sophisticated roll-on/roll-off equipment; lighters carried onboard ships; forms of containerisation; mobile landing ramps; bow and stern doors and ramps; floating dock ships –these and many other features of today's marine scene were there at the beaches of Normandy in June 1944.[1]

Again the basic tools of today–electronics, computers, the cavity magnetron and radar, jet engines, gas turbines, full-scale ship welding, these and many others were either brought into being or practicality by the pressures of war. The base from which the revolution could develop had been established–just as the Victorian base was established in 1830 to 1860.

Afterwards, when recovery had really started, the vastly increased use of the internal combustion engine and of oil for transport, heating and petro-chemicals, coupled with the rise in living standards of many of the peoples of the world, called for increased trade and for the rapid development of oil and ore carrying ships. Indeed, by 1957 petroleum fuels had reached equality with coal as a source of energy.

At the same time, as an inevitable result of war, inflation and the increased living standards apparent in many countries led to an increase in the cost of labour and a need to reduce its content. Overall the scene was set for change in shipping and marine transport methods, change that in the end was to prove so rapid and so sweeping that it became a revolution.

In a revolution not only are new forms created but old ones die, and one of the most obvious aspects of this revolution was the demise of the classic main line passenger ships. Flourishing at first after the war, they continued to do so right through the decade 1950 to 1960. For example, in 1960 many great liners entered service or were launched–*Orlanza*, 20 000 GRT, for Royal Mail; *Empress of Canada*, 30 000 GRT, for Canadian Pacific; *Leonardo Da Vinci*, 33 000 GRT, for the Italia Line, each only one of a group; *Windsor Castle* and *Rotterdam*, both approaching 40 000 GRT; *Canberra* and *Oriana* both approaching 50 000 GRT; and finally *United States* and *France*, respectively the fastest and longest passenger liners ever built. Apparently an expanding and prosperous scene, yet 10 years later the whole breed was on the way to extinction, killed by the jet aircraft and by modern electronics.

In 1950 on the Atlantic, ships carried three times as many passengers as aircraft, by the mid-50s they were on equal terms but by the mid-1960s ships carried hardly any at all. The simplest of calculations shows how relatively uncompetitive the passenger liner was compared with jet aircraft. A ship carrying perhaps 1500 passengers and making a crossing once a week would require more than 2500 tons of fuel to do so and a crew of say 1000. Even a first generation jet carrying perhaps 120 passengers could make 8 or 9 crossings a week – about 1000 passenger crossings, would require only perhaps 12 crew, use only 20 per cent as much fuel and cost perhaps only 20 per cent as much to buy.

Even allowing for the lower grade fuel used by the liner, fuel, crew and capital costs per passenger crossing were much higher than for the aircraft. The result was the inevitable death of one of the noblest creations of mankind, the great passenger main liner.

This depressing picture is not reflected, however, in much of the world's shipping; indeed not only has its position as the most economic form of transport ever devised been maintained, it has actually improved.

The increased use of oil and gas for heating, transport and petro-chemicals has led to a size and population explosion of the crude-oil tank ship and to the development of new types of tank ships for carrying liquified petroleum and natural gases, the LPG and LNG ships.

In the 1830s, Isambard Brunel pointed out that increasing the size of ships would increase their carrying capacity much faster than it would the power needed to propel them at a given speed. This basic principle is of the utmost importance but

economies of size go far beyond propulsion. Not only does it cost much less per ton carried to build but it costs little more, absolutely, to manage or, indeed, to man a very large tank ship than a relatively small one. Structural economies are possible, too, with increasing size although only up to a point. Structure may be more refined both in layout and detail as size increases while corrosion margins are the same whatever the size.

Tanker sizes began to increase under these natural pressures but quantum jumps occurred at the time of the Suez Canal troubles. The importance of Middle East oil to western countries and to the United States of America had been growing rapidly. With the closure of the Canal, oil carriers had to steam south around Africa – a much longer voyage and also exposed to severe weather conditions. To retain the overall cost per ton carried per voyage size had to be greatly increased; the race to the very large and ultra large crude carriers (VLCC and ULCC) was on.

Something similar happened to ore carriers. The home-produced, relatively high grade, ores upon which the world's metal working industries had been founded, were running out and vast new deposits, usually of lower grade material, had to be tapped. The trouble was that these were generally far away; the same pressures to increase size arose and while large ore carriers have never rivalled tankers in size, they still became vast by pre-war standards. The need to avoid the waste of shipping space and time involved in empty return voyages led to a compromise ship, the OBO (oil/bulk/ore) ship capable of carrying oil one way and ore the other.

In these bulk ships, the revolution was one of size and numbers, not to be underestimated, as it was awe-inspiring, maybe frightening, in its extent. The carriage of general cargo, however, has seen an even more far-reaching revolution, to some extent in size but far more so of type and concept. Increasing labour costs, unit values of goods and cost of ships all put pressure, initially, upon shippers and then upon the world's traders to change out of all recognition the entire method of carrying much of the world's goods.

Normal break-bulk cargo handling is by labour intensive methods which result in a large labour content per ton of goods moved in and out of ships. Furthermore, it is slow. The result was that ships spent half or more of their time in port and only half at sea.[2] Basically, a ship is a transport machine, not a warehouse, and yet for more than half of the life of the general cargo vessel, it was constrained to be a very inefficient warehouse.

Pressure mounted to a point where the entire break bulk dry cargo system was questioned, found wanting, and unitised mechanical handling systems introduced to replace it. The result of this was the container ship and the Ro-Ro vessel – a specialised form of container ship – derivatives of and variations on them, and a total revolution in the world's cargo handling methods. This involved a conversion of outlook recognising that all sea transport, apart from special cargoes, must tend towards bulk carriage, in other words, to handling goods in large quantities by standardised mechanical methods without having to pay regard to the ship and the nature of its cargo.

Another aspect of the post-war world has been the greatly increased use of motor-cars, their shipment between the countries of the world and the overwhelming growth of road transport at the expense of rail. This has led inevitably to a burgeoning growth of Ro-Ro vessels and car ferries. Born on the beaches of Normandy, these types of ship are now familiar everywhere and dominate many short sea routes. Indeed, because of the need to overcome congestion in ports in developing countries, Ro-Ro vessels have become strong competitors even on some long-range international routes.

Furthermore, the great increase in the size of oil tankers and ore carriers, the size of the unitised vessels replacing break-bulk cargo vessels and the way that such cargo is carried, the advent of the various types of Ro-Ro vessels and the domination of road transport have all meant the scrapping of most of the infra-structure upon which former types of shipping depended. Many classic ports such as Liverpool and London have declined rapidly, new ports and new facilities in the old ports replacing entire port systems.

The entry of new operators and of third world countries has upset patterns and methods and in many cases both their willingness to consider new ideas and, indeed, sometimes ignorance of the best ways of working to old ideas has led to the consideration and adoption of new *avant-garde* methods. The spur to the established operators has been considerable and has helped their ready acceptance of new systems and methods, an acceptance which might have been inconceivable in 1950.

Finally and above all, the revolution reflects the fact that ships are no longer an end in themselves as a means of transporting goods. They have become part of integrated transport systems, a trend which must develop increasingly in the future. The result is that in 1980, much of the shipping scene has not really evolved from that of 1950 – it is the result of 30 years of revolution. In some cases, an increase in size has called for a totally new technology to permit it, in others, the development of methods for carrying goods and of designing the ships to do it which are totally new and have replaced the systems of the 1950s. Previously unheard of cargoes such as cryogenic liquids are now carried and much shipping effort goes into that post-war phenomenon, the offshore oil industry. Lastly, and sadly, the great classic liner, like the large sailing vessel, has become part of marine history.

The concept of unitisation

As mentioned, the handling of cargo by break-bulk methods became increasingly expensive after the war as hourly labour costs increased and with them the cost of ships. The direct cost of the labour per ton of cargo handled was excessive and the slowness of the methods meant that ships were often tied up in port for 50 or 60 per cent of the year.[3] As ship speeds increased so, unfortunately, did this unproductive proportion of their lives.

Typically, cargo would arrive at a port, mainly by rail but also by road, and be unloaded into warehouses where it would be sorted out for ship and destination. Most of the ships loading such cargo would carry their own gear although ports such as London provided efficient quayside cranes. Cargo would be handled by dockers gangs, usually one or two to a hatch, and sorted into 2- to 5-ton lots, placed in cargo nets or slings and then loaded through rather small hatches into the holds. Stowage would be under the supervision of the First Officer and, to prevent shifting, cargo would be packed tightly in the lower holds and the 'tween decks, dunnage being placed between items where necessary. Much of this cargo would be perishable and had to be protected from rain and snow. Thus, the hatches would be shut when the weather was inclement, although cargo tents with openings through which the cargo was loaded could be used in some cases.

A similar process took place at the other end of the voyage, except that here, in most cases, unloading was by the ship's own gear, typically consisting of derricks with steam or electric winches. These were generally rigged in Union or Liverpool purchase making, in effect, cranes of 2- to 5-tons lifting capability. The system was full of delays. While a reasonable rate for working a hatch apart from bad weather would be 10 tons per hour per gang of eight or ten men, considerable delays would occur even during this time; opening and closing hatches, refreshment breaks, weather delays, dunnage and re-stowing delays, each accounted for about 4 per cent each of the time so that overall only 80 per cent of working hours were actually worked. Similarly, during the whole time that a ship was in port less than a third was spent as working hours so the actual productive time moving cargo was relatively small. Really large break bulk carriers were impractical because of the relatively long periods they would have to spend in port.

In this system it is necessary in many cases to crate goods to protect them from damage and pilferage but, even so, the relatively crude methods of handling, including the use of spikes by dockers, results in a high rate of breakages and loss and being inherently open to pilferage. This system had operated for around 100 years prior to 1950 and still operates today. Expensive in labour costs and time, potentially damaging from a cargo point of view, it has been replaced, to a large extent, by unitisation.

In detail, handling cargo by unitised methods is complex and technical but in concept simple. Basically, it allows standard bulk handling methods to be applied to heterogeneous cargo. Once this is done, it is possible to increase the size of ships and thus make the concomitant benefits available.

Unitisation, in essence, is the breaking down, or alternatively the synthesis up, of goods into standardised units that can be handled by mechanised and possibly automated equipment. As break-bulk, drums of paint, wool bales, cars, crates of canned goods, cement bags, machine tools and so on all have to be packaged, crated and handled in different ways and stowed differently in the ships themselves, but all can go in containers which can be handled in one standardised manner no matter what is inside them.

As with all such technical revolutions it is the infra-structure that determines whether and when it can take place. Brunel's *Great Eastern* failed not because of technical deficiencies but because the ship was too large for the day and the ability to provide passengers in thousands at a time simply did not exist. The ship could not even be dry docked, she had to be dried out in tidal harbours on grids. Similarly, to have introduced wide body jets in 1950 would have led to commercial failure – enough passengers could not be obtained, suitable airports, fuelling systems, etc, simply were not available.

Thus, the first steps towards unitisation were, in the main, tentative. Probably the first containers ever built and to reach a ship were the brainchild of 'the little giant', I.K.Brunel, who introduced them on the Vale of Neath railway in 1841. Cubical iron boxes 1.42 metres inside, each containing about $2\frac{1}{2}$ tons of coal, four fitted in each truck and the whole scheme was introduced on a large scale in order to carry friable coal to Swansea Docks. At the docks machinery was provided to lower each box into the hold of the ship, although it was not left there, the bottom was opened and the coal deposited. This example, though primitive, nevertheless illustrates how cargo can be protected by containers and how standardised transport and lifting plant can be used.[4]

The introduction of true unitisation is probably to the credit of the United States Government which organised a considerable research programme during the Second World War into means for unitising ocean-borne cargoes. This work was aimed mainly at containers but like the early Brunel ones they were comparatively small. Unlike Brunel, they overlooked the need to interlink with standardised land transport. The British Railway Companies had experimented before the war with boxes which could be put on railway flats and which were therefore in themselves true transport containers. With rounded tops, however, they could be regarded more as demountable railway waggons than as stackable containers.

Perhaps the first post-war use of containers was by the United Steamship Company of Copenhagen, which built two small ships in 1950, actually called 'container ships', for a door-to-door transport service via Copenhagen and other ports.

Previously cargo, such as ale from Copenhagen Breweries, was manhandled crate by crate from trucks into the holds of coasters. The United system permitted the loading of a container with 72 crates in less than 2 minutes, into single holds 34 metres in length with large hatches thus allowing a fairly clear drop-in. The ships were only 58 metres in length and 550 tons DWT and although advanced in concept were small and specialised, and did not lead direct to worldwide development. The other early form of unitisation was to load and strap down goods onto small standardised loading platforms and in turn load these pallets onto ships. Again, this development mainly originated in Scandinavia.

However, the true father of containerised unitisation was Malcolm MacLean of the United States – not a shipowner but a man whose business interests were mainly in highway trucking and thus in the overall transportation of goods from a customer's premises to the ultimate destination. The standard method was hauling trailers by highway tractors between points in the eastern United States. Highway travel is relatively expensive, especially in labour, and MacLean acquired a steamship company in order to carry trailers by sea wherever possible to cut down road mileage. This was a complete break with tradition: what MacLean was doing was to provide ships simply as links in a transportation system. The traditional concept of a ship transport system with subsidiary ones at either end never concerned him, his ships simply became mobile bridges in the highway system and the cargo remained in its highway trailers all the way.

In 1956, MacLean fitted two tankers with platforms above the tank deck for carrying 35 ft trailer vans which were detachable from their chassis. Operated between New York and Houston, Texas, the experiment showed the way to building roll-on/roll-off trailer ships. Also, and more important, it led to the full development of the lift-on/lift-off principle and the conversion next year of a cargo vessel, *Gateway City*, to be the world's first true container ship and to be followed by nine sisters. In one brilliant leap, MacLean produced an entirely new type of ship, which has changed little in principle and not really much in detail ever since. Containers, rectangular steel boxes, were stowed in vertically aligned cells in the ship, each cell bounded by vertical guides which prevented the stacks from falling over. Of course, the boxes had to be strong enough to be stacked anything up to seven or eight high and were fitted with corner castings with holes into which locking fittings could be inserted. The containers could be lifted by a gantry crane of 27 tonnes capacity from which suspended a frame with twist lock grips which entered the castings and locked to them.

These cranes, running on hatch coaming rails, could plumb all the container cells and had folding overside extensions so the boxes could be lifted from or dropped onto shoreside trucks. Deck level sponsons extended the tracks right to the end of the cargo spaces and special flip guides were developed to spot the lifting frame onto the containers.

This ship had a capacity of two hundred and twenty-six 35 ft containers and could be turned round in one day by its two gantry cranes – previously with break bulk this would have taken weeks. An immediately obvious advantage showed up once the system was in full operation – handling damage and pilferage were reduced drastically. This system, both in basic design and detail, is virtually unchanged in all container ships today.

Other American owners followed, particularly Matson, running to Hawaii from the United States West Coast, and Grace Line, running to South America. However, each operation had its own sizes

The congestion of a break-bulk berth.
Photo: Port of London Authority

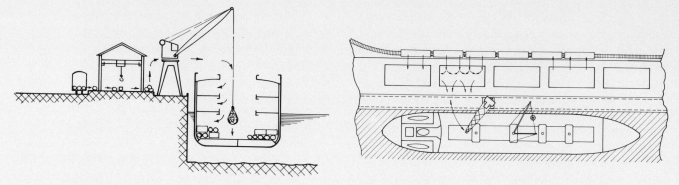

Break-bulk handling, showing spasmodic cargo flow from rail to ship.

of container and was self-contained and independent. Interchangeability was impossible, as was international trade with containers consigned as cargo to other operators. Furthermore, the first ships had to be self-contained with their own big and heavy gantry cranes because no ports had the requisite unloading capabilities.

Again, militating against the spread of container unitisation was the lack of infra-structure. A conventional port required warehouses close to the quays in which break-bulk goods could be stored. This is the opposite to what a container port requires. Here, containers are 'stuffed' away from the port, perhaps in the customer's factory, perhaps in a specialised depot inland. What is required at the ship is a wide open space in which these containers, perhaps still on their trailers, can be assembled and stowed ready for shuffling and sorting prior to lifting aboard the ship.

Many people watched these developments with interest and, indeed, bated breath, seeing a potential explosion of development–it came. The detonator was the American Standards Association, which adopted container size standards in 1961 and 1962, in turn adopted by the International Standards Organ-

isation, ISO, in 1965. It is to the great credit of MacLean that the key patents for the container corner fittings and the mating twist lock grips were released free to the world in the interests of further standardisation.

What could now be achieved was international, interservice handling of box cargo without any interest in the contents. The standard ISO sizes are based upon an 8 ft by 8 ft cross-section and a 20 ft length module. There are 10, 20 and 40 ft lengths available, the standard box being the 20. It was now possible, theoretically, to load an entire ship by numerically controlled gantry cranes, although for practical purposes this is not usually done. In one jump, MacLean and the Standards Organisations had transformed all the paint tins, radio sets, machine tools, canned goods, furniture and what have you, that moved over the world's trade into one commodity: rectangular boxes.

The motivation to introduce container unitisation once it had been shown to be successful was overwhelming. High labour costs, low utilisation of valuable ships and mounting pressure on ports all told heavily against the existing system. An added attraction was that the steadily increasing competition from

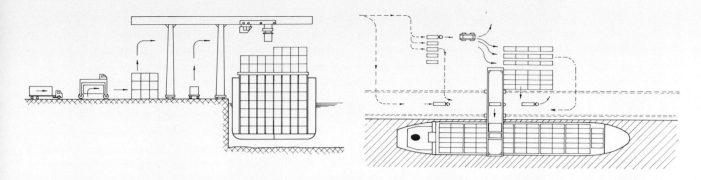

Unitisation, showing smooth flow of cargo from motorway (and railway) to ship.

developing countries in the classic break-bulk trades, using second-hand tonnage and cheap labour, could be confronted by a much more efficient and economic method depending upon large capital resources which these competitors simply did not have. Furthermore, such competition was unlikely to be able to marshal the sheer organisational and technical capability to operate a complicated unitised system, leaving the field open to those who could.

It sounds simple now but the changes required in the infra-structure of the world's ports were of daunting magnitude. A typical loading scene in a 1950 port (page 11) is amplified by diagrams (page 12) showing the typical flow of cargo into a port and to the ship. By comparison, a typical large container port requires an entirely different type of flow. The organisation of a cargo takes place away from the port, which is no longer an end in itself. The flow into the container port and into the ship is interrupted as little as possible (above).

What this change produced has been described by a consortium Line, Overseas Containers Ltd.[5] The first long-range, deep-sea trade, cellular container ship built by any shipowner went into service with this Company in February 1969. The ship, 227

metres in length and carrying fifteen hundred 20ft boxes, was one of a class of six 21.5-knot vessels. A second class, following not long afterwards, was bigger and faster – 290 metres in length carrying 2500 TEU (twenty equivalent units) at a speed of 26 knots.

By the time this system was operating fully, it was apparent that the rate of cargo handling in port had been speeded up by more than ten times with a third of the labour. Furthermore, the cost of cargo damage and loss was reduced to about 10 per cent of that in the break bulk system and the entire fleet operated with 10 per cent of the number of crew of the conventional ships to carry the same ton mileage per annum. This was even more of a revolution than that in break-bulk cargo carrying following the introduction of really efficient steam engines, graphically described in earlier volumes in this series.

The individual ships were as startlingly different from their predecessors as were the two systems. Typical cargo liners of 1950, 1955 and 1965 show that while there was a development of type, it was modest. Size and speed did not show much change although an increase was apparent, culminating in fast cargo liners such as the *Ben Loyal* with service speeds of 20 knots.

In 1950, *Kenuta* of Pacific Steam Navigation for the South American trade was typical of the time. Engines amidships, turbine propelled, *Kenuta* was a ship of 16 knots, 156 metres long, carrying around 11 000 tons of break-bulk cargo. With five holds, cargo handling was by electric winches and derricks, half a dozen of 10 tons, the remainder 5 tons. A 50-ton derrick was fitted. The hatches were small, No.2 being the largest at 15.5 metres long by 6.4 broad. Nos.3, 4 and 5 were only 10.6 metres long. A curious feature was that weather deck covers were a mixture of mechanical steel and hatch board and beam. Machinery was the well-tried, single reduction geared reaction turbine, 9400 horsepower supplied with steam at 30 BAR and 400°C. Well finished, of mixed welded/riveted construction, such excellent ships were still essentially developed pre-war designs.

In 1955 the position was little different. Typical ships were *Arafura*, a 14-knots vessel built for the Australian service, and the 16.5-knot *Nudea* of British India for the India route. Again, engines and houses amidships, again similar machinery and cargo handling gear. Both ships now had sliding steel-covers on all their weather hatches—the experimental period was over. The hatches themselves remained small. Crews were large, 60 to 70 in all, and each ship probably spent at least one day in port for one at sea.

By 1960, recognisable modern features were apparent—machinery and deckhouses were moving aft, totally aft at first only in tramp tonnage. Hydraulic cranes were replacing derricks and the steam turbine had been almost eliminated by the exhaust turbo-charged 2-stroke direct-drive diesel. The modern heavy lift derrick was not uncommon, even up to 180 tons safe working load. Hatches remained single and about 7 metres wide but were generally longer than before.

The successor was very different. Long-range container ships are generally described as belonging to a particular generation, MacLean's ships being the first. The second generation ships of 1969 to 1970 vintage were around 1500 TEU and 21 knots, taking over, for example, the cargo services to Australia. Two or three years later the third generation ships made their debut, for example, *Tokyo Bay* of Over-

The evolution of long-range container ships

	2nd generation *Encounter Bay*	3rd generation *Tokyo Bay*	3rd generation *Sealand Maclean*	4th generation *Table Bay*
LOA (m)	227	290	288	258
Breadth (m)	30.6	32.3	32.2	32.3
Draft (m) (normal)	9.14	10.7	9.14	12.00
Deadweight (tons)	21 750	34 570	20 050	41 600
Displacement (tons)	36 000	58 900	43 050	66 000
TEU	1 500	2 500	about 2 000	2 436
Service Speed	21.5 knots	26 knots	30 knots	23 knots
Machinery	Single screw geared turbine	Twin screw geared turbine 81 000 hp 63 BAR 510°C 370 tons per day	Twin screw geared turbine 120 000 hp, 614 tons per day	Twin screw 8 cylinder turbocharged charged 2 cycle diesels, 51 000 hp, 210 tons per day
	(re-engined diesel 1980)	(re-engined diesel 1980)	(re-engined diesel 1980)	

Southampton container port and cable ship terminal. Note the space required around the berths.
Photo: Overseas Containers Ltd

seas Containers Ltd. Carrying 2500 TEU at 26 knots, these ships were excelled by the *Sea Land Maclean* – a fitting name – and her seven sisters. Comparative particulars in the table (page 14) are instructive.

With the size and speed of the new container ships, and above all the small amount of time spent in port, express round-the-world services became an attractive possibility, especially in the context of groups of long-range liner companies acting in concert – ignoring nationality – thus ensuring the continuity of cargo flow so necessary for these immensely expensive

ships and systems, and such services rapidly established themselves. The ships were limited in breadth by the Panama Canal at 32.3 metres breadth (105 ft) and are interesting successors to the large passenger liners formerly operating such routes. *Tokyo Bay*, for example, is of almost exactly the same dimensions as the liner *United States* and yet she is only one of many such ships.

The third generation ship reached a peak of speed unlikely to be repeated. Entering service around the time of the first round of OPEC oil price rises, they were badly caught by exorbitant fuel bills. Slow steaming was the result with a loss of annual ton miles as their fine forms gave low lifting capacity reserve. *Sea Land Maclean*, at a block coefficient of 0.54, and *Tokyo Bay* at 0.60, simply do not have the lifting capability of *Table Bay* at 0.66. Even slow steaming was unsatisfactory due to poor machinery efficiency at part load and both these groups have been re-engined with diesel plants.

Table Bay is representative of the long-range container ships of the 1980s. As with the third generation, breadth is tied to Panama Canal limits and the overall layout is similar. Compared with a cargo liner of the fifties, *Table Bay* has under 60 per cent of its crew, at capacity load can transport twelve times as much per annum and although 5 knots faster, is only two-thirds of the total horsepower of ships of the same total carrying capacity. This is progress indeed, and once again illustrates the benefits of size and cargo handling sophistication.

These giants will be built infrequently as even major traffic flows can be covered by a few ships. By early 1980 the average container ship being built was 13 to 14000 tons DWT and only a few large main liners were on order. At rather smaller sizes, however, eleven 26000-ton ships were being built for Taiwan and no less than forty-four ships of 22000 DWT for the United States, the country that started it all and which was on the whole a latecomer to the major expansion. Fast, sophisticated, highly automated and even, in their way, handsome, these ships are the true inheritors of the glamour of the cargo and passenger liners on the long-range routes.

Containers can be loaded on and off other than vertically. Essentially, loading endwise or horizontally results in the roll-on/roll-off ships – Ro-Ro. Probably the first such were tank landing ships, the LST 1s, the

Kenuta, a typical break-bulk cargo liner of the 1950s.
Photo: Skyfotos

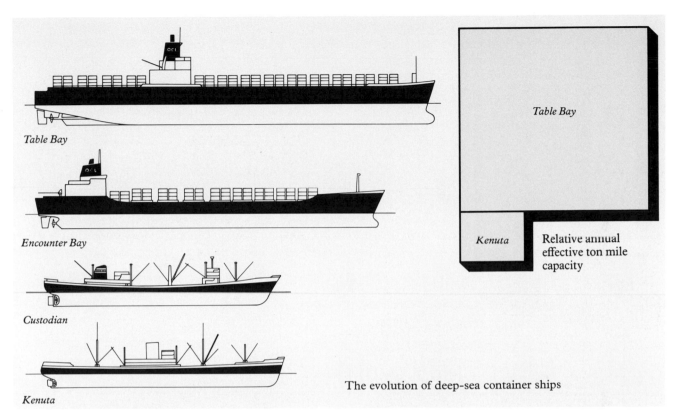

Table Bay

Encounter Bay

Custodian

Kenuta

Table Bay

Kenuta   Relative annual
effective ton mile
capacity

The evolution of deep-sea container ships

Boxer Class, built for the Royal Navy during the early part of the Second World War.[6] These, of course, also had a limited beach landing capability and the world's first purpose-built Ro-Ro ship intended solely for deep-water operation was *Comet*, built by the United States Military Sea Transport Service in 1958. The main vehicle deck was equipped with a stern ramp and two side ports, ramps on either sides, with internal ramps to other decks. Thus, after entering the ship, vehicles could proceed to other decks.

However, *Comet* was anticipated in Britain by the coastal operations of the Atlantic Steam Navigation Company. Founded by Colonel Frank Bustard, it acquired three tank landing ships in 1946 to operate Ro-Ro services between Preston and Northern Ireland and between Tilbury and Antwerp. Over the next nine years the service built up to seven vessels of this type, 106 metres long, carrying 60–80 vehicles at 13 knots or up to 200 motor-cars. The terminals, too, were born of the war – using Mulberry Harbour pontoons and bridges. By 1957 some 40,000 vehicles were carried annually. Finally, *Bardic Ferry* was built for the Atlantic Steam Navigation Company – a true short seas Ro-Ro ferry, 103 metres long, carrying 1300 DWT at 14 knots. This ship, launched in

Custodian, a typical high-grade cargo liner of 1960.
Note the Stulken heavy lift derrick. Photo: *The Motor Ship*

1957, had 1500 square metres of garage space and could carry 50 trucks and 20 cars.

The break bulk cargo liner required around 1.7 to 2.3 cubic metres of stowage per ton of cargo carried. This figure more than doubled for the container ship but modern Ro-Ro ships needed and offered more than five times as much space. Coupled with the horizontal access, this meant that the entire concept of such ships differed from their predecessors.

Normally, the main vehicle deck is the freeboard deck so that the bow and stern and side doors must be above that level. Access to other decks must clearly be by ramps or lifts arranged so as not to interfere too much with cargo stowage. Basically, the true Ro-Ro vessel accepts its cargo on wheels and leaves it there. The trailers or trucks can be road-worthy vehicles or special small-wheeled low-loaders. Alternatively, containers can be lifted from the trolleys and stowed, usually by sidelift operating forklift trucks.

Cardigan Bay, one of a class of five container ships that belong to Overseas Containers Ltd and operate between Europe and the Far East.
Photo: Overseas Containers Ltd

Whatever the system, it is clear there must be a great deal of spare, one hesitates to say wasted, space to permit movement and to accept the wheels and the space around and above them.

For short sea routes, straight-through loading helps to economise both space and time and hence bow visor doors are nearly *de rigeur*. On deep-sea long-range routes, there is not the same pressure on speed of turn-round and, furthermore, the much larger dimensions of the ships, especially breadth, allow vehicles to be turned and stowed for stern unloading – so these are normally stern loaders only.

Vehicles board by ramps and originally by straight bow and stern ones needing end access from a quay. The development of the angled stern ramp and, even more, the slewing ramp, which can land either to port or starboard, has made such ships capable of working wheeled cargo at speed on and off almost any soundly constructed quay.

The deep-sea Ro-Ro ship is now mature and impressive. In mid-1979 the top end of the range is exemplified by the *Lillouet*; 230 metres in length and $32\frac{1}{4}$ metres breadth (again, the Panama Canal limitation), this impressive ship carries a deadweight of 34 000 tons on a draft of 11 metres at $21\frac{1}{2}$ knots. With two cargo decks, there is a slewing ramp at the stern and internal ramps to all decks.

Finally, these two types have come together in one of the most flourishing modern developments – the multi-purpose ship. Smaller, generally 150 to 170 metres in length, 15–20 000 tons deadweight, these vessels are usually fitted with angled shore access ramps, multiple cargo decks, internal ramps and flush hatch covers on the weather deck allowing the

The *Baco-liner*, one of the latest types of barge carrier, which loads through twin bow doors.
Photo: Thyssen Nordseewerke GmbH

carriage of either vehicles, trailers or boxes both on the weather deck and in the hold. They are a mixture of container, Ro-Ro and even sometimes break bulk ship. While complicated, sophisticated and expensive, they have immense earning capability. The Bo-Ro liner developed in Scandinavia is particularly versatile, capable of carrying bulk/oil/Ro-Ro.

A typical voyage for such a vessel illustrates this. Loading 5000 tons of cargo in the Far East, including mobile cranes, motor-cars, containers, etc, at rates varying from 300 tons per hour for containers to 1000 tons for the vehicles, the ship was unloaded in North-West Europe. There, nearly 10000 tons of oil cargo were lifted for a short coastal feeder trip. After discharging this, 10000 tons of forest products were then loaded on trailers at nearly 700 tons per hour. This was in turn unloaded in Belgium where 700 motor-cars were taken on, together with 9000 tons of fuel oil in Amsterdam and the whole of the cars and fuel cargo delivered to Scandinavia.

Unit cargoes can be carried in a third and totally different way in barge carriers. The first manifestation was a unique vessel, the *Connector*, built in Britain in 1850. With a number of discrete sections, hinged together so that individual holds could be left off or picked up at different ports, the power plant and crew could be almost continuously at sea. This concept is used today in the modern barge trains that ply rivers such as the Mississippi and, indeed, by railways everywhere. However, the technology of the day was not adequate and the ship did not lead to a line of development.

The next step was the LSD (landing ship dock), again an Admiralty design of the Second World War. Cargo was carried in landing craft and the ship flooded down by ballasting to allow them to float out or into the hold. LSDs needed no harbour facilities: the landing craft ran to and fro from the coast.

Once again, the real development of this new type of ship was in America where the so-called LASH ship (lighter aboard ship) and SEEBEE concepts were developed. Such ships have developed along two lines. In one, springing from the LSD, barges are floated in or out of a vessel, which can be ballasted down to a deep draft. Loading is usually at the stern although recently bow-loading vessels have entered service. The other type lifts the barges by means of cranes or elevator platforms at the stern, usually between two large extensions of the upper levels of the stern or in a lifting recess in the entire stern.

The pioneer LASH ships were built with broad transom sterns and a pair of heavy cantilever structures extending aft of the hull forming a docking area and crane runway. Deckhouses are near the bow leaving the entire deck clear. The machinery uptakes are carried up the side of the ship clear of the path of the crane, a fairly standard feature in many Ro-Ro and container ships. The main deck has a series of very wide hatches with single-piece hatch covers through which the lighters are handled. The travelling gantry crane in these ships has a lifting capacity of about 500 tons, can lift the lighters out of the water and load them into any part of the ship.

Barges are of several types, perhaps unfortunately so remembering the standardisation of the container ship. First, the basic Mississippi barge, made up into gigantic trains on that river, is 59.44 metres long, 10.67 metres broad and 3.35 deep, carrying 1360 tons of cargo. SEEBEE barges are 29.72 by 10.67 by 3.81 metres carrying 847 tons. These, it can be seen, are half-size Mississippi barges. The Capri barge is almost the same size at 30.48 by 10.67 by 4.40 metres lifting 1000 tons. Then the standard LASH barge is 18.75 by 9.5 by 4 metres carrying 370 tons of cargo but obtainable in double and treble length versions.

It seems unfortunate that there should be this variety of sizes, further complicated by the entry of Russia into this field with the Danube barge, 24 by

9.5 by 5 metres and 800 tons deadweight, which is also used by the low-loading *Baco-Liner*.

Barge carriers have developed rapidly into very large and sophisticated vessels of immense cost. The *China Clipper* – a Mississippi barge carrier – is 292 metres long overall by 32.3 metres breadth, of 10.7 metres draft ballasting down to 17.3 metres to load the barges. Loaded, this ship carries 40000 tons deadweight including 14 of these large barges, 1000 containers and a considerable quantity of Ro-Ro cargo at 20 knots – a far cry from the wartime LSD!

These systems make possible large-scale door-to-door cargo transport between inland river ports even though they may be one or more oceans apart. For example, the Mississippi and Rhine Systems have been linked by LASH and other lighters since 1969. Usually, the lighters themselves must be loaded break bulk, but an attractive variant of the system is to use lighters with container sub-loads. Where there is a long river system not navigable by the mother ship, the lighter-onboard-ship system must be inherently slower than a true container or Ro-Ro system. The wasted space and weight too is considerable, a ton of lighter being carried for every 5 tons of cargo. Nevertheless, there is no doubt that in some places the lighter carrying unitised system is very attractive and economic, particularly when linking inland ports up large river systems.

So, in the 15 years since ISO introduced world standards for containers, the domination of cargo trades by the cargo liner and its derivatives, one that had lasted a century, has been destroyed. As swift as the elimination of the passenger liner, at least it was by new types of ship and not by totally alien machines.

Of course, the conventional break-bulk ship lives on, forming the backbone of the fleet of many developing countries. With the unitisation of main trade routes it might be thought that it would be on a decay curve leading to eventual extinction. This is not so. Some countries, for example the USSR, have been building steadily and while in 1977 break-bulk tonnage on world order was $4\frac{1}{2}$ times that of container ships, it is still $1\frac{3}{4}$ times as much. Furthermore, the Multiflex concept – able to carry almost anything, including containers, reasonably efficiently – will give the cargo liner a renewed lease of life.

Nevertheless, while there will always be some place for break-bulk ships, it must be recognised that this dry cargo tonnage is largely centred round containers and that much of the cargo carried by these ships is, and increasingly will be, in boxes, albeit handled by ordinary cranes and not stored in cells.

In 1980 about 1000 large cellular container ships and Ro-Ro ships are in service. Of these two thirds are container ships. Ro-Ro ships have only 20 per cent of the overall container loading capacity but such is the speed of loading and unloading that capacity is restored to balance with the container ships.

The investments required are, of course, enormous. A container ship capable of carrying 2500 TEU costs around 80 million dollars in 1980 and the three sets of containers to go with it a further 30 million. The terminals with their enormous space requirements and expensive handling machinery represent similarly large investments – shore to ship cranes at perhaps 3 million dollars each, terminal gantry at 1, specialised forklift trucks at half a million each; investment at this level has to some extent excluded developing countries from participation. Some ports deal with more than 1 million TEU per annum and in 1980 New York comfortably exceeded 2 million. The cost of equipping such ports is enormous.

So all in all in just a few years the cargo carrying picture has dissolved, recrystallised and formed into one that will be with us for many years. It seems unlikely that such a revolution will affect it again within our lifetime.

Barge carriers as sophisticated as the LASH ship are like ports in themselves.
Photo: Port of London Authority

Oil tankers and bulk carriers

While method has changed most in dry cargo carrying it is in ships intended to carry liquids and solids in bulk that the greatest development in size has taken place in the last 25 to 30 years. Many modern ships are very large but the oil tank ship in particular has developed in a way which would have staggered the imagination of pre-war designers, builders and operators.

The real development of tankers has taken place almost wholly in this century. In 1930, tankers represented perhaps 40 per cent of the world's shipping. This dropped during the depression and rose again to just over 31 per cent at the outbreak of the Second World War. The percentage rose steadily from about 20 per cent immediately thereafter to 41 per cent in 1949 and over 50 per cent in 1950. While this reflected a doubling of oil production between 1939 and 1950, right into the fifties the size and type of tankers showed little change.

In 1950, however, new refineries were being built throughout the world, in Britain, for example, at Shellhaven and Fawley. These were to have profound effects upon the size of vessel which could be employed. Hitherto the tendency was to refine at source, such as at the large refinery at Abadan in Iran, and to distribute, in effect, products. This had advantages at the time in labour costs but was politically vulnerable and technically inflexible as only one feed stock crude was available at each refinery. Crudes vary; some are light, others heavy, some waxy, others not. Ideally, refineries need to blend crudes for efficient operation. The new ones were to be at destination – at the point of consumption – and hence only one commodity was to be transported, namely crude oil and this could come from several sources.

When distributing products, conditions at the discharging ports limited the size of oil tankers – the Shell Group alone loaded at 25 ports, discharged at ten times as many. The change was reflected immediately in the type of tanker ordered to service the new refineries.

A typical ship was *Velutina* of Shell, 186 metres length between perpendiculars, 24.5 metres breadth and carrying about 28 000 tons on 10.4 metres service draft at a speed of 15 knots. The 13 000 horsepower machinery was supplied with steam from three boilers and the layout was of classical type, with midships deckhouse and 33 cargo tanks arranged three abreast.

Over the next five or six years, the pattern of movement of oil by sea was well illustrated on a BP map. The importance of the Middle East even then is seen clearly, as something over one third of the world's tanker fleet was engaged in delivering its oil to Europe and only about 20 per cent in local supply of the East Coast of the USA and Canada. No oil was reaching America or Europe around the Cape of Good Hope. By 1955, vessels of 32 000 DWT were quite common and ships of 45 and 60 000 tons were on order. The thinking behind this growth was well appreciated even in 1950. Figures published by an American tanker operator in 1949 showed that at a constant service speed of 15 knots on a 6000 mile voyage, the operating cost per thousand ton miles of a 32 000-ton ship was half that of a 12 000-ton one.

Sizes now began to increase steadily with Britain still building well over half the world's tanker tonnage, launching the world's largest tanker, *Spyros Niarchos*, of 47 500 DWT in 1955. Tankers had reached nearly 60 per cent of the tonnage launched in each year and development was given a sharp spur by the nationalisation of the Suez Canal and the short war that followed it.

When the Suez Canal was first closed in 1956, a transit draft of 10.4 metres was possible allowing ships rather larger than *Velutina* through loaded. It had been hoped that development of the Canal would to some extent keep pace with the growth of ships and that the optimum would be a ballast voyage out through the Canal, loaded back via the Cape. However, that was not to be for a long time, certainly not politically. Up to this time tankers of 35 000 DWT loaded had been able to transit the Canal: now, suddenly, they had to make for Europe around the Cape of Good Hope, increasing the 6500 mile voyage via the Canal by nearly 80 per cent. With the ships of the day the extra cost of transport per ton of oil was £2.50. Furthermore, Britain alone would require 7 m DWT of extra tanker capacity.

So, to keep overall costs under control, a sharp drop in the cost per ton mile was essential, and it was achieved by a sudden quantum jump in the size of crude tankers. By 1959, the first 100 000 DWT crude carrier had been built – *Universe Apollo* of 104 000 tons – followed shortly afterwards by a slightly larger sister. These ships, 275 metres long and 41 metres broad, drew 14.6 metres and achieved 15 knots in service on 23 000 horsepower.

By the end of 1959, tankers of 40 000 DWT and over accounted for one eighth of the world's carrying capacity, although such ships had hardly existed five years before. More impressive, two thirds of all tanker tonnage on order was over 40 000 DWT. This alone shows the impact of the new refineries and, equally important, the swing away from carriage of Middle East oil through the Canal.

While there were some 40 tankers of over 50 000 DWT afloat by the end of 1960, nearly all of them steamships, the average size of the world's tankers was still only 19 000 DWT. However, in an age of fan-

Velutina, one of the first large crude carriers but only 28 000 DWT. Photo: Skyfotos

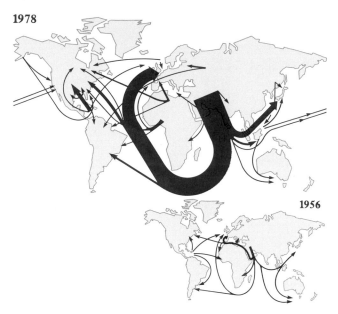

1978

1956

The dramatic effect of the Suez Canal closure on main oil movements. Courtesy: British Petroleum Co. Ltd

tastic technological capability under economic pressure, the world was about to be presented with new initials, VLCC and ULCC—the very large and the ultra large crude carriers were at hand. In 1962 the *Nissho Maru* of 130 000 DWT went into service and by the mid-sixties had been passed by ships of 150 and 206 000 DWT. The year 1965 saw the first British built 100 000-ton tanker while the United States had constructed one of 108 000 tons in 1962. By 1965 there were 44 tankers exceeding 100 000 DWT afloat. The age of the super tanker had arrived. In 1968 the *Universe Ireland* of Gulf Oil reached 327 000 DWT, and three years later a 370 000 DWT ship was afloat. The half-million-ton tanker was in sight in 1973 with the construction of two sister ships for Globtik of 477 000 DWT. Today the palm is held by two sisters—*Batillus* and *Bellamy* of 554 000 DWT. Monsters 414 metres long, 63 metres broad, drawing over 15

fathoms of water—they weigh 630 000 tons loaded.

This was still an era of cheap oil and of cheap transport, too. The extraordinary efficiency of sea transportation is nowhere better shown than by the VLCC. In 1970 the cost of transporting a ton of oil from the Arabian Gulf to Europe was exactly £1. Remembering the *extra* cost in 1956, this figure is a remarkable tribute to the economies of size. The subsequent explosion in ordering was largely due to the imbalance between cost and demand of both oil and its transport as in 1970 charter rates were as high as £8 per ton, i.e. eight times the cost of transportation.

With charters available under these terms and highly favourable credit terms on offer from shipyards, a vast ordering programme commenced, in many cases by people and organisations hitherto little connected with shipping. To illustrate the temptation, a 250 000 DWT VLCC for delivery in 1973 was estimated to cost 28 million dollars. Such a ship might be expected to make 4.8 voyages per annum lifting about 1.2 million tons of oil on which a profit of £7 per ton could be made. Thus, the first cost of the ship could be repaid within two years.

By 1970, the distribution of the world's fleet of large tankers showed a number of interesting features (see top diagram page 27), in particular the tentative introduction of a particular size of ship and then its sudden rapid population explosion. Smaller sizes peak off just as the larger sizes begin and the smooth progression is striking. In 1970, of the 63 ships of 200 000 DWT and over, Britain owned more than one third, a picture which was soon to change.

The subsequent growth in tanker tonnage was extraordinary until the bubble was pricked by the OPEC price rises of 1973. The bottom diagram on page 27 shows the tonnage on order from 1970 to 1980 in two groups, under 150 000 tons and over. The fantastic situation immediately prior to the OPEC rises

The start of the explosive growth in tanker sizes

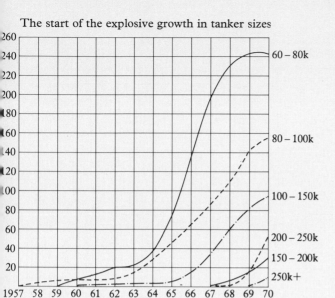

Large Tankers

The rise and fall of the tanker boom

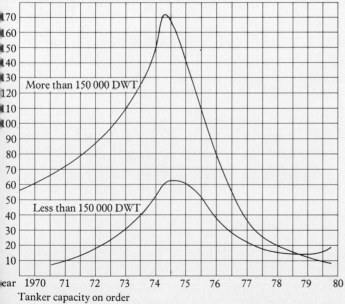

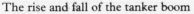

Tanker capacity on order

Sources (top and bottom): *Fairplay* and *The Motorship*

was potentially catastrophic and almost certainly would have produced a tanker slump anyway. Tonnage was being ordered at a rate far exceeding the sum of natural wastage and the growth necessary to service increased oil consumption. Such a situation has always been a recipe for slump and disaster. This there was, as the diagram indeed shows.

Consider two years, 1976 and 1977. In the former, 1 million tons deadweight of VLCCs per month were scrapped and 6 million tons per month of orders cancelled. Also, approximately 100 000 DWT per month were destroyed in casualties! In 1977 the world tanker tonnage totalled 321 million DWT and there were 56 million tons on order. The scrapping rate continued at something like three to four times the normal level and a large number of new ships were laid up, some straight from the shipyards. Others absorbed excess capacity by steaming at low speeds, 12 knots instead of the 15 to 16 of which they were capable. In that year, 59 tankers between 100 and 200 000 DWT were laid up, together with an incredible 62 ships each in excess of 200 000 DWT. The wasted human effort and capital involved is staggering and a sad commentary upon the greed and lack of foresight that led to the tanker ordering boom.

At the end of the decade and of our period, the world's tanker fleet totals about 330 million DWT, more than 65 per cent of which consists of ships of over 200 000 tons: nearly 800 ships in all, each one, it must be remembered, bigger than the 'Queens'. Second-hand VLCCs can be acquired for a little as 7 or 8 million dollars and the Japanese are currently using more than 20 such ships as static oil storage tanks – an uneasy parallel with the fate of some large passenger liners such as *Michelangelo* and *Raffaelo*, the flag ships of the Italian fleet now used as dormitory ships in the Middle East.

By 1982, it is anticipated that tankers of 250 000 DWT will be able to transit the Suez Canal loaded. At present they can do so in ballast, and ships of 150000 tons can transit loaded. This has a balancing favourable effect on the cost of transport but, on the other hand, will tend to produce a surplus of capacity. In view of the political instability of the Middle East, owners may well prefer to continue to use the Cape route.

However, it would be unreasonable and unjust to overlook what the large tankers have done for mankind in the last 15 years. The landed price of oil would be much higher if it were not for the economic transportation provided by these giant ships. Their safety record appals some but, on analysis, not by virtue of the number of casualties but simply because of the sheer magnitude of any one. In fact, per ship their record is excellent, but of course they constitute a very large fleet and each one holds in its tanks the seeds of a major ecological disaster.

Batillus, 554000 tons DWT, being lightened by *Drupa*, 70000 tons DWT, itself two and a half times the carrying capacity of *Velutina* of 1950.
Photo: Shell

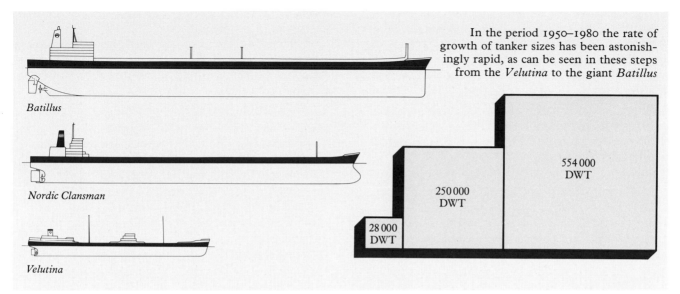

Batillus

Nordic Clansman

Velutina

In the period 1950–1980 the rate of growth of tanker sizes has been astonishingly rapid, as can be seen in these steps from the *Velutina* to the giant *Batillus*

28 000 DWT

250 000 DWT

554 000 DWT

Technically, they are a remarkable achievement by the shipbuilders and naval architects of this generation. Deficiencies may exist but they are not inherent and are mainly due to economic pressures often imposed by shipowners. It can be argued that they should be fitted one and all with twin engines or at least twin boilers if turbine, probably with twin screws and certainly with duplicated steering gears.

The current regulatory situation produced by IMCO (Intergovernmental Maritime Consultative Organisation) goes much further, introducing new initials such as CBT, SBT, IGS and COW! SBT is simply segregated ballast tanks and CBT clean ones. COW is crude oil washing and IGS inert gas systems, filling tanks with incombustible gases. As far as new tankers are concerned, ships whose keels are laid in 1980 and whose contracts have been placed in the last half of 1979 are fully affected. The larger ships of over 20000 DWT must be fitted with SBT or COW and IGS and the tanks must be protectively located. Existing tankers will be required to conform progressively

with some of these requirements. Of course, these measures will reduce the available tanker capacity and tend to restore the balance of tonnage/demand. At the same time they increase the cost of transportation.

This is not the place to discuss in detail the technicalities and implications of these measures, but inert gas systems clearly reduce the danger of explosions by preventing explosive gas mixtures building up in oil tanks. Segregated and clean ballast tank systems imply a reduction of the carrying capacity of the tanks for a given size of hull and in themselves will have an economic impact in reducing the available deadweight tonnage of tanker fleets. Crude oil washing is an alternative to SBT. There is no doubt that an entirely new generation of tankers will be seen in the 1980s. Indeed, some progressive owners have already anticipated these changes and ordered ships. Some have already been completed, which conform with the new ideas.

Finally, it is instructive to compare the largest

tanker built in 1950, *Velutina*, with the largest afloat today. This ship is 1¾ knots faster than was *Velutina* but taking them both at 15 knots, 1 horsepower propels about 13 tons of *Batillus* and under 3 of *Velutina*.

Each member of the crew represents nearly 13 000 tons of cargo in *Batillus* and only 500 tons in *Velutina*. It takes little calculation to appreciate the true economies of scale achieved in a quarter of a century of crude carrier evolution. Unlike *Velutina* and the bulk of the world's tankers, *Batillus* has twin screws and twin rudders, an increasing tendency for ULCCs.

Each propeller is driven by a 32 000 horsepower steam turbine, fed by a single boiler, a real improvement on the typical VLCC layout with a single main boiler. Cargo tanks are in three rows abreast, each about 21 metres wide and the total length of the tanks is 326 metres, themselves longer than the *Queen Elizabeth*. A typical centreline tank can carry about 30 000 tons of oil, around the total deadweight of *Velutina*.

No longer is the cargo system manually controlled as in earlier crude carriers: today in a control room abaft the bridge, the positions of all valves are indicated, as are the levels in tanks, and control is remotely operated. Level alarms can be set for all tanks, and the whole operation of cargo handling by the duty officer can be automated by a computer which not only manages valves but performs the necessary loading stress calculations.

Inerting of the tanks is essential today and, as is normal with steam tankers, gas is taken from the boiler uptakes, scrubbed, cooled and fed to the tanks with no more than 4 per cent oxygen content.

Such ships are controlled from a central navigation machinery control centre on the bridge. Cargo control, machinery control and navigation areas are instrumented to a most sophisticated level with remote indicators, alarms, mimic diagrams of all systems, remote controls and monitors. The machinery spaces are scanned by fully manoeuvrable television projectors.

Bulk carriers of loose materials, whether of grain or other materials such as coal, are close relations of oil carriers, especially of the crude carriers. In general proportions and hydrodynamics, they are virtually identical, although generally of rather smaller size. Indeed today there is a large class of such ships which are both oil tankers and bulk carriers, the so-called OBOs, oil/bulk/ore ships. The development of the bulk carrier, as a distinct type apart from break bulk cargo ships and ore tankers, is longstanding but as with the other bulk vessels, there has been an extraordinary growth of size and numbers in the last 25 to 30 years.

One of the characteristics of oil tankers, especially crude carriers, is that they tend to make only one leg of their voyage loaded, the other being in ballast. Bulk carriers are very often in a similar situation and this led to the concept of multi-purpose vessels which could carry oil one way and various bulk cargoes the other. An early example of this type of ship in 1950, the *Porjus*, 162 metres long by 20.7 broad, carried 15 600 tons deadweight on 8.667 metres draft. Seven thousand horsepower and 14 knots, *Porjus* carried ore on the centreline in dedicated holds with oil in the wings and in the very deep double bottom beneath the ore hold.

As in the case of oil tankers, the growth race was started by Universe Tank Ships and in 1955 this company built *Ore Transport* of 60 000 DWT, 230 metres in length, 35 metres breadth – much the largest ore carrier in the world. At this point ore carrier development tended to split into two streams. The very large ships were clearly necessary for really long-range transportation of ore and bulk cargoes in quantity, but a considerable market existed, for example, in Europe for much smaller vessels and this was underlined by the publication of standards for major importers such as the British steel industry. A typical ship built to suit their requirements in 1955 was 16 000 tons deadweight, 166 metres long, with draft limited to 8.54 metres.

The development of this type became quite standard, 20 000 DWT, around 165 metres in length and of set arrangement with deckhouses and machinery aft offering about 16 knots from 10 000 to 11 000 h.p. The big ships continued to grow, spurred by the development of, for example, the Japanese steel industry, which simply was not content with 20 000-ton packages of ore as was the British. The straightforward ore carrier specifically aimed at iron ore and coal grew until the equivalent of the VLCC was the standard 150 000 DWT ore ship.

The OBO type also grew and there is no doubt that the theory behind it was attractive. In practice it is questionable whether these ships have fulfilled their promise. While return cargoes can be, and have been, obtained, the ships are more expensive than either tankers or bulk carriers, the amount of work involved in changing their function, cleaning ore holds to receive oil and so on, is costly, and considerable

doubts have been thrown upon their inherent safety – certainly their record leaves much to be desired. The sinister disappearance of the very large OBO, *Berg Istra* and, some time later, of her sister cannot but be discouraging, especially to the insurance market. The impact of the new IMCO Regulations, SBT, CBT, etc, will further complicate an already specialised design.

A major problem with the design of these ships has been sealing and electrically earthing the hatch covers and preventing leaks. Apart from ships such as *Berg Istra* that have disappeared, there have been numerous explosions aboard OBOs due to electrostatic discharges in ore holds/tanks which were not yet fully inerted and gas freed.

There is doubt today whether the OBO will in fact survive, although such ships are still being built. A good example is the *Norrland*, an even more specialised ship called a PROBO (product/oil/bulk/ore carrier). This ship may well be among the last of the line but certainly it is of extreme flexibility. The tank

Porjus, a predecessor of the modern OBO ships.
Photo: Skyfotos

arrangements, together with the piping, pumping and tank-cleaning features, enable *Norrland* to carry oil product cargoes as well as crude oil, ore and grain and other bulk cargoes. Two hundred and thirty metres in length, 45.5 broad with a design draft of 12.8 metres and a scantling draft of 16.1, *Norrland* can, at maximum, carry nearly 131000 tons.

How such a vessel operates is interesting. Carrying light ore, oil products or light grain, the ship uses shallow draft but with oil or heavy ore, operates at scantling draft, while normal crude oil and heavy grain cargoes can be carried at a draft intermediate between the two. The arrangement of the holds is similar to that of the *Porjus* of 1950 but the wing spaces now are not oil tanks but used for segregated water ballast. Thus the oil is carried in the central

An impressive view of *Norrland*, a modern PROBO.
Photo: Gotaverken Group

portion with hatch covers, which is also used for ore when that is the cargo.

Straightforward bulk carriers continue to be built in quantity, but the very large ships of 150000 DWT and thereabouts are uncommon. In 1977, production of OBOS amounted to 5.4 million DWT spread over 50 ships averaging 108000 tons each. Bulkers, on the other hand, amounted to 780 ships totaling 30 million DWT and averaging 38600 tons each. In 1978 the orders for both types of ship had halved. OBOS and ore/oil ships dropped to 22 ships averaging 115000 tons each and bulkers to 390 ships averaging 36000 tons each.

In late 1979, the position had settled somewhat with 20 ore/oil and OBOS on order averaging just over 100000 tons each while there were some 314 bulkers on the books at 36000 DWT each. It can be seen, therefore, that these ships have now stabilised, approximately one fifth of bulk ship capacity being represented by ore/oil and OBOS, the ships in themselves being just over 100000 DWT. Straightforward bulk carriers, however, are generally around the 36000 ton size, some 3–400 of which are built throughout the world each year. Bulk carriers are a stable and normally profitable part of the shipping scene, particularly in their element when large grain movements have to be made. They have an assured future, and while overtonnaging did take place, especially at the end of the tanker boom, it did not reach levels which would automatically produce a real slump.

So, from 1950 to 1980, ships such as *Porjus* have grown from about 15–16000 DWT to about seven times as much. Normal straight bulk carriers have grown, on average, by a factor not much more than 2, although there are many which are twenty times the deadweight of the 1950 ships. There has been a revolution but probably bulk carriers represent one of the less spectacular parts of it.

Ferries and cruise ships

For more than a hundred years, power-driven passenger ships of all sizes served mankind, crossing oceans, narrow seas and straits on regular and fast schedules. From large Atlantic liners to cross-channel packets they developed steadily, and this pattern persisted until well into the 1950s. Then, with the introduction of really efficient air transport, it withered and disappeared in a few years. Passenger ships and ferries themselves did not disappear, however, but changed radically as counter-balancing factors appeared. The increasing affluence of Western society and the leisure available to it, together with the dominance of the motor-car, have led, in their respective spheres, to a widespread revival of shipping on the short sea ferry routes and to the building of new and quite large liners devoted solely to cruising.

On the ferry routes, typical passenger ships built after the Second World War were *Mona's Isle* representative of vessels on the Irish Sea routes, and *Avalon* of British Rail for the Harwich/Hook of Holland route, one of the last pure passenger ships to be built for use around the British coast. Such ships would be recognised instantly by the shipping world of 50 years ago: 110–120 metres long, powered by steam turbines of modest temperature and pressure, weatherly, fairly low built, they were not very different from the ships built shortly after the First World War. Intended to link with railways, in effect they did not recognise the existence of the motor-car. Passengers were expected to arrive by train and any cars were shipped as deck cargo.

In the early 1950s, car ferries began to make an appearance. Typical of these was the ill-fated *Princess Victoria*, lost in the great storm of 1953. Carrying vehicles above her bulkhead deck but with a forecastle at the forward end of it, the ship had an open entry stern closed only by shallow gates. Such ships were an immediate success as people discovered the convenience and the enjoyment of taking their cars with them, avoiding humping baggage and providing real mobility at each end of the voyage. The loss of the *Princess Victoria* led to the development of fully watertight, closeable stern doors and general development to the fitting of multiple-tier car decks. The French ferry *Compiègne* only 5 years later was an excellent example of the new breed. One hundred and fifteen metres long, with capacity for 164 cars at three levels, the ship embodied all the basic features of current car ferries. With these features, the car ferry was set on a road which had led to a remarkable growth of routes and ships all round the coasts of Western Europe, Japan and of North America.

To the man in the street, this is the most familiar aspect of shipping. In essence, a car ferry is a cross-channel vessel fitted with a vehicle deck at the previous weather deck level, probably with a superimposed vehicle deck above that or, alternatively, a portable one and with accommodation decks above that. Vehicle access is through a door at the stern which is usually of upward lifting and perhaps folding type. Many such vessels today have a visor bow which permits straight through driving and parking. This hinges at the level of the forecastle and lifts upwards, exposing a tunnel into the forward end of the ship, generally closed by a hingeing watertight door.

Such ferries, of course, are not autonomous and must be provided with extensive shore operating facilities. The general type is the linkspan or bridge hinged at one end and resting on the ship at the other, lifted and adjusted by a portal frame which straddles it. Most short sea routes experience considerable tidal variations and a considerable degree of adjustment on such linkspans is thus a necessity. An alternative is some form of floating linkspan, again hinged at one end to the shore but hinged at the other to a pontoon of suitable type which may be used as the landing platform for vehicles from the vessel. In some cases, such ships enter tidal docks where the quay freeboard is constant and where a very simple shore facility suffices.

An interesting variant was introduced by the Isle of Man Steam Packet Company in the early sixties. Faced with a lack of linkspans anywhere on its various routes, the company produced an ingenious spiral ramp at the stern with exits at various levels. Thus, whatever the tidal height, the relevant exit could be used via a portable bridge.

These linkspans and shore terminals proliferated throughout the 1950s and 1960s all round the coasts of Europe and Japan. By 1970, there were nearly 200 ferry services operating round the coasts of Europe, many connecting the British Isles with North-Western European countries. Other areas of intensive operation were between the Scandinavian countries and in the Mediterranean, Adriatic and Aegean Seas.

Since then the pace has increased, as has the size of the ships. The changes in ferry routes, particularly over the last 10 to 15 years, have in themselves amounted to a revolution. Some of the ships that have been built are of a size and sophistication undreamt of in 1950. The accolade must go to *Finnjet*, operating on the Helsinki to Travemunde route and intended to reduce the crossing time by half to 22 hours. *Finnjet* is 213 metres long overall, displaces

Avalon, a latterday North Sea passenger ship.
Photo: British Rail

Mona's Isle, an Irish Sea passenger ferry of the 50s, retired in 1980. Photo: Isle of Man Steam Packet Co. Ltd

Finnjet, the ultimate development to date of the overnight passenger/car ferry.
Photo: Wartsila Helsinki Shipyard

16 500 tons, carries over 1500 passengers and up to 350 cars or a mix of cars and commercial vehicles, all at a maximum speed in excess of 30 knots provided by two 37 500 horsepower aircraft gas turbines. *Finnjet* does the work of three conventional ships and offers very high standards of accommodation, quietness and convenience.

Smaller, but still large, *Dana Anglia* is typical of the best practice on the routes from Northern Europe to Britain: 153 metres length overall and capable of a typical 21 knots, she carries 1250 passengers and up to 470 cars. Deck space is what is sold by such vessels, hence the high slab-sided deckhouses of ships such as *Finnjet* and *Dana Anglia*. Ferries as a type are now generally rather unbeautiful but some designers do produce quite good-looking ships such as *Dana Anglia*. The latter provides a total stowage area for vehicles of 5100 square metres disposed on two decks and accessed by a stern door and a bow visor. Typical machinery for such vessels are medium-speed diesels running at 4–500 RPM, geared to controllable pitch propellers. Variants such as *Finnjet*'s gas turbines and New Zealand Rail's diesel electric, are few and far between. The vast bulk of ferries today fit this more or less standardised type of propulsion.

Like *Finnjet*, and indeed *Avalon*, *Dana Anglia* makes an overnight voyage and sleeping accommodation has to be provided for passengers, but on the classic cross-channel day routes, ferries have also increased in size. Entering service recently, *Spirit of Free Enterprise* (front endpaper) is 132 metres in length, 8200 tons gross register, carries 1300 passengers, sixty 12-metres trailers and 60 cars. This ship is unusual in being triple screw, with a fourth bow propeller conferring unusual operational flexibility, and has 24 000 horsepower giving a service speed of 22 knots. Generally, cars and coaches are carried on the upper vehicle deck and freight vehicles on the main deck. Her owners have always been independently minded in design matters, and *Spirit of Free Enterprise* is unusual in having side swinging bow and stern doors. Unloading is simultaneous on two levels and in four lanes, thus forcing port authorities to provide two-tier ramps. There is much to be said for the triple screw layout and for straight-through access.

Such ships exemplify the underlying trends in modern shipping. Designed for very rapid turnround, for carrying right across the spectrum of what is offered, in this case passengers, cars, vans, heavy trailers and trucks, they are very much in line with the thinking of the multi-flex ship, the Bo-Ro ship, and so on.

In 1950 who would have dreamed that the ferry routes would have been shared with 40- and 50-knot ships whose hulls were not even in contact with the water? Yet this is the case; passengers are being ferried across the English Channel and the Irish Sea at these speeds in hovercraft and hydrofoils whose origins are not at all nautical, but rather aeronautical. The hovercraft, in particular, has made a significant impact on carryings across the English Channel. One company alone carried over a million passengers in 1977 and nearly $\frac{1}{4}$ million vehicles and, what is more, at a profit. Certainly, the hovercraft must be accepted as a real and viable part of the ferry revolution.

The short sea ferry and cross-channel ship has come a long way. Happily it has not died out. Instead, it flourishes exceedingly in its multi-purpose form and also happily its large sister, the passenger liner, has seen a re-birth in a different and flourishing form.

In their dying throes, many of the main line deep-sea passenger liners turned to cruising, either under their own flags or those of Greece and the USSR. A number of old Cunarders fly the hammer and sickle, and the last and longest of the true North Atlantic liners, *France*, has been re-fitted as the cruise liner *Norway*. Denuded of half her propulsion, she is now a twin-screw ship, like her competitor *Queen Elizabeth II*, which was built, however, with cruising in mind as well as some main line Atlantic work. Straightforward passenger liners are not generally suitable for cruising and only those built with some cruising in mind, such as the *Queen Elizabeth II*, *Canberra*, *Oriana*, etc, are viable. However, the last 10 to 15 years has seen a remarkable revival of passenger liners built purely for cruising. For example, in 1979 no less than five new cruise liners were ordered, culminating in a 31 000 GRT vessel due to enter service at the end of 1982. Two hundred and ten metres long, this ship will be able to take 1400 passengers on three-week cruises to the Caribbean. A rather similar vessel is being built for operation under the American flag, 200 metres long carrying 1420 passengers in some 500 cabins, this ship again will cruise to the Caribbean, indeed the bulk of the tonnage under construction is intended for this service, lifting passengers out of United States ports.

It may be asked why the classic passenger liner, even refurbished, is not suitable for cruising. Today,

Dana Anglia, a typical highly developed North Sea ferry optimized for deck space. Photo: DFDS A/S

the cruising public is sophisticated and highly critical of deficiencies. Especially is this so of the American market; passengers require the very best in service, food and entertainment, in accommodation and recreation facilities, including equipment for shore-going. The older passenger ships, built without these requirements in mind, simply do not have the amount of open deck space, the swimming pools, restaurants, games rooms and bars provided by purpose-built cruise ships. Again, most of these older passenger ships have been mixed class with a large number of lower grade cabins – an embarrassment to the cruise operator rather than an asset. This is not to say that the classic passenger liner cannot be converted suitably for cruising, but generally when this is so the ship has been built with this in mind. An example is the P&O conversion of the Swedish *Kungsholm*, 26 700 GRT, built as an Atlantic liner in 1966, to the cruise liner *Sea Princess*. Even though *Kungsholm* had been designed for some cruising, P&O spent a great deal of money on her conversion to current standards.

P&O, of course, operate successfully two very large cruise liners, *Oriana* and *Canberra*, of about 48 000 GRT, and perhaps this has encouraged the Norwegian operator Kloster to buy and convert *France* of 66 000 GRT.

To illustrate what has to be done to such a ship, the sun, boat and verandah decks were all lengthened to provide adequate open deck space. Extra luxury cabins were built on the sun deck while the public rooms on the verandah were rebuilt with a church, cafés, a night club, boutiques and bars.

Cruising in the sunshine requires extensive swimming pools in open decks. *France's* existing one was extended and a new one built on the promenade deck together with a big outdoor restaurant. For getting ashore two large 25-metre shore tenders are carried, each capable of lifting 400 passengers. To minimise the use of tugs, three bow thrusters and two stern

thrusters, taking a total of 11 000 horsepower, have been fitted. Extensive alterations have been made to the main machinery, including the eradication of the forward engine room and altering the remaining turbines to provide the mere 40 000 horsepower needed at 21 knots.

New cruise liners built from scratch are nowadays of distinctly futuristic appearance, with overhanging bows, very built-up superstructures and observation lounges and spaces above the wheelhouse. Quietness and lack of vibration are essential features of this type of ship for obvious reasons. It is true that generally the ships are not fast, 21 to 22 knots being all that is required. Absorbing the power required without vibration is not difficult, but even so some operators have adopted highly skewed propellers with each blade shaped like a sickle in order to ease its entry into any uneven flow behind the hull. The accommodation is designed with the same thoughts in mind. For example, on *Cunard Countess*, an 18 000 GRT Cunard cruiser, the steel cabin decks are glued to a 30 mm insulating layer in turn laid on the ship's structural decks. The cabin bulkheads and linings are mounted directly onto this floating floor, thus isolating the spaces. Again, to reduce the impact of the environment, such vessels are always heavily roll-stabilised, usually with fin type units.

Cunard Countess is typical of this new type of liner, as is her accommodation. A ten-deck ship, eight are made available to passengers. Uppermost is the observation deck and below that the sun deck. This is centred amidships on a lido area with a large swimming pool, and forward of that is an observation lounge incorporating a casino and dance floor. The forward end of the bridge deck below contains the wheelhouse and navigation spaces, and aft of that open space for passengers. The boat deck below incorporates the main lounge with a stage, dance floor and open bar, and aft a night club and cinema followed by more open deck space. There are some luxury cabins on this deck with similar cabins on the deck below with the main restaurant and another cinema.

Convenience and efficiency of disembarkation are essential for these ships, and No.4 deck has a large disembarking area including shops, shore excursion offices and information bureaux. Cabins are located throughout this deck and on the decks below.

The new generation of liners built for cruising will be very similar. For example, the *Bremen*, a 27 000 GRT liner due for completion at the end of 1981, provides 315 cabins for 600 or so passengers and will cruise out of North Europe to Spitzbergen, through the Baltic, Mediterranean and Black Sea, to both East and West Coasts of Africa, to the Caribbean and South America and to the Far East.

The one-time absolute dependence of the world upon passenger liners for inter-continental travel has gone irrevocably, but without doubt their mantle will be carried for many years yet by this new, flourishing and impressive breed depending for its livelihood upon leisure and recreation and the wealth to enjoy them.

Cruise ships, such as *Cunard Conquest*, are the successors of the passenger liners. Photo: Scandia Photo

Newcomers

There is no doubt that the world shipping scene of the last 20 years has been dominated by the growth in size and number of tankers, particularly crude carriers, and by the development and growth of unitised dry cargo carrying. Tankers have represented an explosive growth of an already established technology with, of course, the infusion of much new knowledge and thinking. Container vessels are a new development, pioneered in the 1950s, but they have, like the tanker, simply developed in size and numbers in the last 10 years. The same can be said of bulk carriers. Indeed, of the ships described earlier, *Velutina* is recognisable in *Batillus*, *Porjus* in *Norrland*, and *Gateway City* in *Tokyo Bay*.

On the other hand, there are important sectors of tonnage afloat today which have few recognisable roots in the beginning of our era. Gas carriers of all types, specialised car carriers and heavy lift ships, lifting dock ships, dynamically positionable drilling ships, pan type cable ships and many others were all undreamt of commercially only this short time ago.

Perhaps the most striking of these are the liquid natural gas carriers, vast expensive vessels carrying a product which to most shipowners of 1950 would have seemed more at home in science fiction than in forecasts of responsible ship owning in the next quarter century.

In terms, too, of sheer technical achievement, it is arguable that the accolade must go to the liquid natural gas (LNG) ship. Its cargo, methane with some ethane, forms a large part of the natural gas available in many parts of the world. An excellent fuel but very light, it has hitherto been unusable unless within piping distance of sizeable markets. It is a light gas, explosive when mixed with air, cannot be liquefied by pressure alone and when carried as a refrigerated liquid, boils at $-161°$C!

In countries such as the United States and the Soviet Union, it has formed a large part of the energy supply by virtue of being on the spot and easily available. It is an excellent fuel but the vast natural gas resources available, for example in the Gulf areas of the Middle East, in Algeria and the West Coast of Australia, in the past had to be left in the ground or flared off when recovering oil. For example, in 1958 some 60000 million cubic feet of waste gas was flared off and it was estimated at the beginning of 1978 that something like the equivalent of $2\frac{1}{2}$ million barrels per day of oil was flared as gas, equivalent to about 75 per cent of the gas consumption of Western Europe.

The heavier petroleum gases such as butane and propane are easily liquefied by pressure alone and during the 1950s, small LPG ships of 300 to 1000 tons were constructed quite widely. This type of ship is still common today, of course, and relies upon carrying the liquid gas in pressure vessels which generally protrude above the deck.

However, for large vessels, LPG carried under pressure is not economic, and by 1960 carrying these gases refrigerated was an accomplished fact, a ship of some 9000 tons deadweight having been constructed in Scandinavia with a 20000-ton vessel under construction in Japan. By 1965, the largest LPG carrier had reached 36000 cubic metres volume and nearly 30000 tons cargo deadweight. In Europe, these ships tended to be more specialised, for example, vessels such as the Norwegian *Havfrost* were often dual propane or ammonia carriers. On a length of 141 metres the ship could carry 6000 long tons of propane or, alternatively, 7200 tons of ammonia. This cargo was carried at atmospheric pressure at about −48°C for propane and −33°C for ammonia. Ship structural steel is brittle at these temperatures and hence the tanks are not integral with ship's hull but built as separate units insulated both from the hull and from ambient conditions.

Natural gas is, however, quite a different story. At normal temperatures it is supercritical, in other words, it cannot be liquefied by pressure unless below −82°C, but must be carried refrigerated. It is unlikely that a combination of refrigeration and pressure will be economic, so LNG carriers generally carry their cargo in purely cryogenic form. The attractions of liquefying methane are considerable. If liquefied, it reduces in volume by 630 times to a specific gravity of 0.42, rather less than half that of oil. Butane, on the other hand, can be liquefied even at 39°C by a pressure of only 2.5 bar and propane at the same temperature by 12 bar. As LNG boils at −161°C, containing it clearly poses a severe problem. Fortunately, aluminium alloys improve in their mechanical

Havfrost, a ship to carry two difficult cargoes, propane and ammonia. Photo: Skyfotos

qualities as temperature is lowered and are suitable for tank materials, as is 9 per cent nickel steel and some other alloy steels in this range. Tanks can be constructed free standing and supported from the ship's structure by load-bearing insulation or on insulated stools, the sides being surrounded by non-load-bearing insulation.

The first LNG cargoes were carried in a converted American CI type cargo vessel, *Methane Pioneer*, in aluminium tanks insulated from the structure by balsa wood. Problems abounded. Aluminium contracts 50 mm in 15 metres between normal temperatures and that of LNG, and this had to be allowed for.

Piping and valves had to be developed for the cryogenic cargo and no doubt this was assisted by experience gained from the space and missile programmes which had to deal with similar temperatures. The cargo would be continually boiling: even in a large LNG carrier, a boil-off of more than $\frac{1}{4}$ per cent per day of the cargo is to be expected.

Methane Pioneer was arranged to carry 2200 tons of LNG, shipped from the owners' site in Louisiana to Canvey Island on the Thames where a reception terminal had been built. The first cargo arrived in February 1959 and seven further cargoes were delivered over one year. No troubles were experienced,

A typical LNG carrier, such as *El Paso Howard Boyd*, carries 125 000 cubic metres of liquid methane at −161° C.
Photo: Newport News Shipbuilding and Dry Dock Co.

everything worked as intended and the way ahead was clear.

The first commercial operations were from Algeria to Britain for which two ships were built in the United Kingdom. Much larger than *Methane Pioneer*, 188 metres overall, with a service speed of 17¼ knots, carrying 12 000 tons of LNG, the first, the *Methane Princess*, arrived at Canvey Island in October, 1964, her sister ship two weeks later, boil-off from the cargo providing much of the fuel for propulsion. This was the true birth of a new breed of ships, which must become increasingly important as time goes by in spite of their enormous cost.

In July, 1965, a French methanier, the *Jules Verne*, entered service, with 25 000 cubic metres capacity and 13 400 tons deadweight. The tanks were vertical axis cylinders, and the ship also carried Algerian gas, this time to Le Havre. From there on development has been rapid. In 1975, for example, 106 gas carriers, mostly large, were on order from the world's shipyards.

For their part, LPG carriers had grown to monsters of over 100 000 cubic metres capacity, a typical ship, the ESSO *Western Port*, built in France for Exon, being 255 metres overall, with a service speed of nearly 17 knots. Such ships, however, are of limited draft compared with oil tankers, in this case not much over 12 metres. Carrying 64 000 tons of cargo at −46°C, this ship is constructed with a complete inner hull throughout the whole length of the cargo section, the space between hulls being sub-divided to take water ballast. The cargo tanks themselves are fundamentally rectangular, each located in a hold on suitable seatings with locating links and anti-floating chocks in case the hold be flooded. The tanks are sub-divided by a centre-line and a transverse bulkhead to prevent 'sloshing'. The space between the inner hull and the tank is filled with perlite insulation, a granular mineral. All empty spaces in the cargo area are filled with inert gas as are the tanks before loading.

LNG carriers tend to be rather larger, a standard size being 125 000 cubic metres, perhaps 280 metres overall, but again with a draft of only about 11 to 12 metres. The *El Paso Howard Boyd* is typical. LNG has a specific gravity of just over 0.4 and LPG of just over 0.6, so for a given weight of cargo the ships are very much bulkier than crude tankers, with high freeboard, typically nearly 30 metres for a 125 000 cubic metre ship.

LNG carrier designers have now settled on three different methods of building and insulating tanks. In one form, typically, six tanks of rectangular shape are installed in much the same way as described above for LPG. Alternatively, tanks may take a spherical form: a number of such ships are in service, again at 125 000 cubic metres or larger, typically with five spherical tanks, these protruding well above the weather deck giving the appearance of an enormous LPG carrier with pressurised tanks. The LNG tanks, however, are at atmospheric pressure. Nearly 37 metres in diameter and built of aluminium, the walls are 2 inches thick and covered with 9 inches of polyurethane insulation and each tank is supported from its horizontal diameter on specially designed stools. In yet another type, the so-called membrane system, the insulation itself carries the hydrostatic load, primary and secondary membranes or skins providing containment of the liquid.

It is fascinating that several such radically different solutions to a basic and immensely difficult problem should have been developed. It is a technical achievement of the first order to carry LNG at all and yet whatever the design type, spherical stressed tanks, rectangular membrane type or rectangular self-supporting tanks, these ships have given remarkably little trouble. Gas carriers will increase in importance, especially LNG carriers, methane forming the bulk of natural gas. Japan imports nearly 25 billion cubic metres of LNG per annum and will import perhaps half as much again by 1985. The trade will call for larger and larger ships: 330000 cubic metre vessels are contemplated, 350 metres long. Curiously, such ships are quite light; the draft of 12–13 metres reflects a loaded displacement of only about 200000 tons.

The safety of LNG carriers has been questioned; clearly, a major collision with such ships would present many dangers, but there are counterbalancing factors. The gas itself is lighter than air, the extreme cold of the cargo is likely to prevent all fire and even if a leak should occur, if penetration to a tank took place in a collision, it might be argued that it might very well seal itself off due to the formation of large quantities of ice. Perhaps more than any other, the LNG carrier epitomises the sheer daring and technical expertise of shipowners and naval architects in the last quarter of this century.

LNG transport suffered from the post-OPEC hiccup just as did all other forms of energy transport. However, by 1978, the world sea-borne trade in LNG reached 20 billion cubic metres per annum and 45 billion by 1980. Seventy-two LNG carriers are in service with an aggregate capacity of over 4 million cubic metres and 26 more are on order. It is anticipated that by 1990 something of the order of 200 billion cubic metres per annum of LNG will be carried by sea. So from 1977 to 1990, there would be approximately a 10-fold increase requiring the construction of 90 ships of the 125000 cubic metre size: truly a new sea-borne industry.

Looking a little like a gas carrier is another product of markets that simply did not exist 25 years ago— the car carrier. In the mid-fifties, controversy raged over shipping space for motor-cars. Manufacturers, especially in the United Kingdom, claimed that shipowners were not interested in the dollar market. The latter riposted that the freight rate would have to be

Opama Maru, the first ocean-going specialised car carrier. Photo: Hitachi Zosen International, S.A.

Young Splendour, a pure car carrier, takes 3000 cars at 21 knots. Photo: Hitachi Zosen International, S.A.

increased by 50 per cent to carry motor-cars and in the end the car companies turned to chartering tonnage themselves. Cars were carried specially crated, enabling several layers to be stowed in holds, and European and Japanese car manufacturers in particular became interested in the building of ships with specially movable car decks and later in specialised car carriers themselves.

Cars are light and not very high and so were wasteful of the space in the vessels of the day. The lack of enthusiasm of the average shipowner is understandable with such cargo stowing at nearly 12 cubic metres to the ton. By 1965, liner companies were fitting portable car decks in many ships, a typical example being the type produced by Barclay Curle. This comprised steel panels fitted in the 'tween decks with portable beams, wood panels fitted in each hatch opening and stowed on the deck panel when not in use. Wires, led from the normal cargo winches, were used for the erection and stowage of the decks, which could be prepared for cars in under an hour. Originally invented in Britain, this system became common during the first half of the 1960s but was replaced eventually by the altogether more efficient specialised car carrier.

The first ocean-going car carrier, the *Opama Maru*, was built in Japan in 1965. Carrying 1200 cars, this vessel set the pattern for future tonnage. Cars were driven directly on and off over a stern ramp and were then lifted up or down to the appropriate deck by an elevator and moved sideways to the final position by a mechanical car shifter.

Another totally new type of ship, the pure car carrier (PCC), had been born and expanded rapidly. In 1970 car carriers had reached 160 metres overall and were capable of carrying over 3000 cars at 21 knots. A typical ship, *Lorita*, belonging to Uglands, carried 3200 motor-cars on nine car decks, all with restricted headroom of 2.52 metres. Loading, however, was not automated as in *Opama Maru* but was via side doors and ramps, side doors from the quay up ramps to each deck, final loading being sideways by forklift truck.

Sometimes called garage ships, pure car carriers expanded rapidly in the 1970s as, indeed, did bulk carriers specially designed or converted to carry cars.

The most popular size of the latter was around 30 to 32 000 DWT, while the garage vessels increased in size to the point where the Panama Canal became a constraint. Such ships can carry 6000 to 7000 vehicles and are generally owned by a small number of Japanese and European shipping companies. Two hundred metres in length, they contain around 50 kilometres of linear car stowage.

By the mid-seventies, these ships had more or less totally replaced the earlier lift-on/lift-off vessels, in which handling tended to damage the cargo. But, like most other classes of tonnage, car carriers suffered from over capacity towards the end of the decade, for instance in 1977 alone, 25 large PCCs were ordered with a capacity approaching 150 000 vehicles. These ships were less inflexible than their forbears, having

Super Servant, a submersible lifting ship capable of lifts of more than 10 000 tons. Photo: Wijsmuller B.V.

light, movable car decks which could be shifted to permit the carriage of commercial vehicles. With a large international movement of new cars likely to continue for many years the car carrier will be an enduring type of vessel.

Another type which has developed beyond recognition in our period is the heavy lift ship. It is true that even before the Second World War there were specialised HL ships but it was the invention of the Stulken derrick–that V-shaped excrescence on so many vessels today–that ushered in a new era. This consists of two angled unstayed posts, with a centrally mounted derrick which can work forward or aft between the posts and generally outboard to about 6 metres with the vessel listed up to 15°. These derricks rapidly reached capacities of more than 400 tons and are still a viable and profitable heavy lift system. Typical of ships using this gear was the *Custodian*, a cargo liner built for the Harrison Line, 146 metres overall with a 110-ton Stulken derrick between Nos.3 and 4 holds (page 18).

In the last 10 years or so, however, entirely new types of heavy lift ship have appeared. These employ a variety of new methods for handling heavy weights drawing from other types such as Ro-Ro ships, LSDs, submersible barges and so on. Many of these are, like aircraft-carriers, asymmetrical, with derricks and deckhouses to one side, generally to starboard. This is a copy of the system adopted for the self-unloading log barges pioneered on the West Coast of North America with cranes and deckhouse to one side and loaded above the deck with logs. By selective heeling they discharge their entire deck cargo sideways over the gunwale.

A typical specialised heavy lift ship, then, may be something over 100 metres in length with, perhaps, two Stulken derricks or the like fitted to starboard, with a Ro-Ro stern entry and a lifting capability of 800 tons.

As an example of the open-minded approach of today's shipowners, two container ships were ingeniously converted to a catamaran capable of a lift of 1200 tons provided by two Stulken derricks located on the starboard side of the port hull. The bridging structure at deck level is matched by a hydrofoil strut under water and thus the vessel has an immense deck area on its beam of 32 metres – again Panamax.

These ships are a new type, but even newer are the semi-submersible heavy lift vessels which follow two lines of descent, the first from the Landing Ship Dock of the Second World War and the second from the type of submersible barge used, for example, to salvage the SS *Great Britain*.

With a conventional heavy lift vessel loading over the side, the large heeling moment must be counteracted by flooding ballast tanks or by a compensating force where a loading foot is extended onto the jetty or ship from which the load is lifted. With really heavy loads, it is preferable to load over the stern, ships having much greater longitudinal than transverse stability. This is the origin of the really heavy lift Ro-Ro ship, the capability of which can be extended by travelling gantry cranes running the length of the ship. The result is not dissimilar to the LASH and See-Bee vessels, the loads, however, boarding from a quay rather than as barges.

Some heavy lifts, however, are so large – drill rigs, for example – that they simply cannot be lifted or rolled onboard. Here, the semi-submersible type of vessel comes into its own. One type is really rather similar to the See-Bee barge carrier. Springing directly from the wartime LSD, these vessels have a long central hold which can be opened, generally, but not always, at its after end, and which, when the vessel is ballasted right down, allows cargoes to be floated in. A specimen cargo might comprise a bucket dredger, a couple of tugs and a dozen barges, all

intended for some inland waterway operation abroad. The barges might well, however, be of pontoon type with bulldozers, earth-moving equipment, etc, on their decks lashed or welded down. Loading is a rapid operation and down time for the equipment is minimised.

The other type of semi-submersible heavy lift vessel like the submersible barges submerges the entire main hull leaving only deck erections above the surface. Some of the earlier barges were totally submersible and required one end brought above the surface to acquire stability before lifting the cargo. This slope is not desirable and later versions retained a forecastle at least which would be above the surface and supply some stability. The semi-submersible self-propelled ships generally have two casings aft-

Dock Express 10, a dock lifting ship capable of 2000-ton lifts. Photo: Bob Fleumer

extended so that they come above the water and a similarly extended forecastle and bridge. Thus they can lift horizontally.

Excellent examples of both type have entered service in the last year of our period. The *Dock Express* ships (below), 152 metres long, are really LSDs with Ro-Ro capability and stern ramps. In the Ro-Ro mode, single piece cargoes of up to 600 tons can be driven onto the vessel through the stern door while two 500-ton gantry cranes running on the sides of the ship and spanning the entire hold handle both hatch covers and cargo and give lift-on/lift-off capability of 1000 tons.

In its final role as a dock ship, the vessel is ballasted down and any floating cargo within the limits— length 116 metres, width 20 metres, draft 5 metres and weight 2000 tons—can be floated into the hold, the stern door closed and lifted out of the water by the de-ballasted ship. Complete jack-up offshore rigs overlapping the sides can be transported by vessels such as this which have a total deadweight of 12 000 tons and a speed of 16 knots.

The other semi-submersible is exemplified by the *Super Servant* (page 44). These vessels are in effect flat barges with a vertically extended forecastle forward and extended wing casings aft. One hundred and thirty-nine metres length overall and 32 metres in breadth (Panamax again) they can be submerged so that the deck is 6 metres below the waterline. The cargo is then loaded by float-on/float-off and as the ship has a deadweight of about 14 000 tons, limits are really only the draft of 6 metres and the unit deck

Photo: Bob Fleumer

Loading a cable magazine into a Pan type cable ship.
Photo: Marine Division, Post Office Telecommunications

loading of 15 tons per square metre. Ships such as these would have been inconceivable 20 years ago.

Pressures to increase capital utilisation and decrease labour costs have forced into being a whole range of new ship types in many different fields. The list is long. An example is the cable repair ship, repairing the spider's web of various cables leaving a major country. Such ships inevitably find themselves loaded with the wrong cable when an urgent repair arises. Normally, unloading and re-loading cable tanks takes weeks, as it is fundamentally a manual operation. The new type of Pan or unitised cable ship (above) loads its cable in large magazines rather as a ciné camera loads film. Weighing 70–100 tons at a time these pans can be pre-loaded with different types of cable and the ship can come in, unload, re-load the new required type and be away again in a matter of hours. During the Northern Hemisphere winter, this can result in one ship performing the work of several and is an excellent example of unitisation of what, on the face of it, would have seemed to be ununitisable.

Twenty-five years ago, ships sorted themselves out neatly into a small number of easily definable types. Under today's pressures anything goes. If a need exists or an opportunity offers, a ship can and probably will be designed and built to fill the gap. It is remarkable that the growth of the VLCC, the introduction of cellular container ships, of LNG carriers, of specialised types such as have just been described, have all been successful from the start. Resources and experience are such that it is very unlikely that the prototypes of a new type of vessel will be lacking technically. In the 1980s, we may well see icebreaking tankers bringing hydrocarbons from the Arctic to North America. Such ships are being designed now and, for example, may well approach 150 000 hp, carry 140 000 m⁷ of LNG and be capable of breaking ice that would stop all ships of today except a few specialised ice-breakers. Even if a new trade sounds difficult, if the economic case is good enough it will be achieved. Indeed, the danger is more that old and well established technologies will become decadent and lessons learnt long ago have to be relearnt.

Modern shipping is often plagued with vibration problems; some Ro-Ro ships have been lost due to openings being improperly closed; VLCCs have suffered horrific accidents through inadequate detail design of components such as steering gears, etc. The lesson perhaps is that the full glare of modern technological capability has been focused on the difficult aspects of design while what is relatively easy has sometimes been given relatively perfunctory attention. It will not be surprising to go on hearing that some ships continue to suffer from problems in quite minor and ostensibly well established detail.

The technology of the revolution

It is difficult to describe the technology that made possible the revolution in merchant shipping because much of it extends so far beyond the realm of shipping itself. In essence, ships have become links in transport systems rather than the system itself. Thus the technology of the infra-structure such as the development of motorways and mass road transport, of air travel and the jet aircraft, of new types of refineries and so on, has had quite as much effect upon the design, shape and numbers of ships as has that of the ships themselves. Staying, nevertheless, within the marine boundary, perhaps the most striking aspect of the changed shipping scene has been the immense growth in the number of ships and in their size. This has meant a corresponding increase in world shipbuilding production capacity, an increase that has unquestionably got out of hand, resulting in massive over-capacity for which the world's shipbuilding industries arc now paying. Technically this expansion was made possible once again by developments originating in the Second World War, when the need to produce ships in quantity was overwhelming and the then conventional methods of production had to go by the board.

In hull construction a dominant role has been played by welded methods of fabrication. All-welded ships were constructed before the war but the immense possibilities offered by welded fabrication for quantity production were first exploited during it. The traditional way to build a ship was to lay a keel, to lay adjacent to it the double bottom, then to erect the frames or ribs and then the plating, decks, bulkheads and so on. This process builds good ships but

is necessarily slow and certainly all work has to be carried out on the confined and restricted berth. If the berth could be used simply as an assembly area then such fabrication could take place in machine shops, under cover, with extensive handling equipment available, thus concentrating a much greater productive effort on each vessel. The net result would be a shorter overall time for construction and an immense reduction in berth time. Shipbuilding berths are limited in number and working area and are expensive, so this so-called prefabrication permitted much greater output than the traditional method of construction.

It was not, however, well suited for riveting. This is a process where each rivet driven is a skilled act, even when hydraulic riveters are used rather than hand hammers. Welding, while skilled, can be broken down into simpler stages and additionally in many cases can be carried out purely mechanically. The flowering of these two techniques was in the immense wartime shipbuilding programmes such as those of the well known and publicised *Liberty* ship, 10 000-ton cargo vessels of simple type, but also in the mass production of warships, such as frigates, destroyers and some types of larger vessels.

When the need came in the 1950s and thereon to expand shipbuilding capacity and the size of ships, these techniques were found to be ideally suitable. As the size of cargo and oil carriers grew, more and more flat plating was involved, and this was obviously suitable for mechanised welding using deep penetration welding machines and automatic cutting and welding plant on a large scale. Thus, the means to build the ships of this period extend directly from the war. This was also the case with the development of electronics and its offspring, particularly the digital computer and numerically-controlled machine tools.

In constructing a large modern ship such as a VLCC, the procedure then is radically different from the production in the past of a large ship such as a Transatlantic liner. Then the ship would certainly be built on a sloping slipway whose declivity provided a gravity launch into the water. Now the tendency is for large ships to be built in building docks, although this is not universal. Such a dock is shallow and is used for production assembly only. It is usually spanned by large travelling cranes of up to several thousand tons lift. There are variants – one large shipyard builds vessels in a covered shed starting with the stern, extruding the vessel from the shed stage by stage until the bow finally leaves the shed and the ship is virtually complete. In another tanker building yard, advantage is taken of the fact that the bulk of the machinery and fitting work is in the stern of the vessel. Sterns are built up from pre-fabricated

A modern shipyard is an assembly plant. Note the flow of prefabricated sections. Photo: Odense Steel Shipyard Ltd

units and fitted with machinery, the machinery being lifted in as soon as the bottom units are in place. A building slip is used and here bows and the tank portions are completed one after the other. As each bow and midships section portion is completed, a stern section is skidded in sideways, attached and the complete ship launched.

In a typical modern shipyard the flow of material for hull construction is simple, logical and kept as straight as possible. Plate is discharged from trucks close to the plate yard and sorted ready for demand. From there the material is taken to straightening rollers, which produce absolute flatness, and is then shot blasted and primed so that there is no chance of it being either dirty, rusty or covered with scale. The clean painted plate then goes direct to the plate shop and the numerically-controlled flame cutters and shearing machines. Bending and rolling is next carried out and the smaller sections and parts are fabricated here. Units of perhaps 40 or 50 tons are taken from this shop direct to the building berth.

The bulk of the work is, however, carried out in a major prefabrication shop which may be laid out in several parallel flowlines. Here, sections which may weigh 100 to 200 tons are completed and loaded on to trailers or air floats and taken to the building berth or to a storage area. If to the former, they are brought within reach of the cranes which then lift them into the berth in the appropriate order.

In fabricating these units, advantage is taken of the fact that a great deal of a modern ship may be split up into flat panel work. The tendency today is to design ships with no sheer on any decks, with no camber on any but the weather deck and with deck-houses of purely rectangular construction. It can be seen that this results in a large proportion of the structure being flat panels—plating with stiffeners on one side.

Especially with very large ships such as tankers and bulk carriers, the cost of steel fabrication is tied closely to the ability to produce panels as cheaply and rapidly as possible. This has resulted in the development of one-sided welding methods. Previously it was necessary to weld one side of the plates and then turn them over and weld the other. With the new system it is possible to complete the operation from one side only. An immensely difficult process to develop, it is now commonplace, accomplished by high output machine welders. Machine welders, incidentally, turn out the quality work of the highest uniform standard.

The attachment of stiffeners is also carried out mechanically in such plants. Plating is curved where necessary either by rolling as at the bilges or by line heating at bow and stern, compared with the older methods of rolling and pressure forming. Line heating exploits the expansion of the metal when hot and its contraction when cold. If a local area is heated considerably it expands, and if the surrounding area is cooler, the local area is then compressed because it cannot expand freely. On cooling it shrinks and pulls the adjacent plating round into a curve. This is the reason for the characteristic 'starved horse' appearance of many welded constructions.

A common technique today is to install machinery on the berth when access is possible without lifting the plant over the sides and decks of a partially completed ship. By installing the machinery at this stage, time and costs are cut, and there is no doubt but that it is a more efficient method, especially when the welfare of the machinery itself is borne in mind. Assembling an engine room in this way could lead to a situation where it cannot be disassembled, in other words, as the ship is built round the machinery it may be difficult to maintain or repair it. Care is taken to avoid this and common practice today is to build large-scale models of engine rooms in advance of the ship as a check. Protection of the machinery before the rest of the ship is assembled round it is a serious problem, and this and other factors have led to the growing use of covered shipyards where the entire ship is assembled inside a building shop isolated from ambient conditions. Steelwork units are still prefabricated outside in the welding shops but assembly is now entirely under cover and all operations can be performed under optimum conditions and the installed machinery protected at all stages. A pioneer of this type of shipyard was the one mentioned earlier which actually moves the ship out of the building assembly hall on rollers, adding to the bow end as the ship is moved. By this means, of course, a much smaller building shop can be employed, but for smaller ships it is becoming commonplace to build totally under cover.

So, the actual arrangement of a shipyard is now quite different, generally building docks instead of slipways, prefabrication of immense sections instead of piecemeal assembly, automated panel production factories supplying the assembly shops and, finally, the construction of the ship and the installation of its machinery under cover and in a different order from that in the older method.

There has been, perhaps, less change on the machinery side. The most common marine propulsion engine today is the direct drive diesel operating usually around 115 to 120 revolutions per minute, although the tendency is to lower revolutions to obtain improved propulsive efficiency and lower fuel consumption. These engines are immense, some of the largest weighing nearly 2000 tons.

The type of slow-speed direct drive diesel engine that has come to the fore is the 2-stroke, exhaust turbocharged, crosshead engine. These are single acting, that is, fuel is burnt on one side of the piston only, and the side thrust of the piston rod is taken on a crosshead which constrains the piston rod to move simply up and down. The connecting rod connects to the crankshaft. Thus the arrangement is very similar to that of the classic reciprocating steam engines which, however, were nearly always double acting, although some latterday engines, such as the uniflow type, were single.

Turbocharging is today nearly always by blowers or compressors driven by gas turbines run from the exhaust gases discharged by the cylinders. These pressure-charge the incoming air. Typically, engines are of uniflow type, that is to say, air is admitted through valves at the top of the cylinder and the fuel is injected similarly, while exhaust takes place through a row of circumferential ports at the end of the stroke. The larger sizes of these engines have a bore of over 1 metre and a stroke approaching 2 metres and run at around 100 revolutions per minute. Latterly, engines have been designed for even lower speeds, of about 90 RPM. To give an idea of scale, a typical large engine with bore 1.05 metres, stroke 1.8 metres running at 105 RPM would develop 4000 horsepower per cylinder and a 12-cylinder version would weigh somewhere around 1600 tons and be nearly 26 metres in length. The overall height would be as much as 14 metres – truly these are 'cathedral' engines.

Steam turbines for the large ships have also developed, current advanced practice being for pressures of well over 100 BAR (1500 lbs/sq. inch) with temperatures in excess of 500° C. These so-called re-heat plants show fuel costs per horsepower mile similar to those of direct drive diesel engines. There is no doubt but that the current tendency is away from steam and towards diesel as shown by the use of two 25 000-horsepower diesel engines of the type described above in the container ship *Table Bay*, while her earlier sister, *Tokyo Bay*, now re-engined, had two 40 000-horsepower steam turbine plants. The current re-engining of steam VLCCs with diesel engines is another example.

However, a further revolution may be on the horizon. Coal is becoming potentially a much cheaper fuel than oil, in spite of its lower calorific content per unit weight and the extra space needed for bunkers. Experiments with new types of boiler, such as the so-called fluidised bed boiler, and with other methods of burning coal, may well lead in coming years to a significant amount of tonnage turning to steam propulsion fired by coal.

As far as smaller ships are concerned, such as Ro-Ro vessels and many of the smaller container ships and so on, there is a marked tendency to standardise on medium/low speed diesels running at approximately 4–500 RPM. Such engines are not of crosshead type and are very often fitted in pairs on a shaft, the necessary gearbox being no great disadvantage as the engines have to be geared down anyway to give suitable propeller revolutions.

A typical large prefabricated unit, the whole of the accommodation unit. Photo: Harland & Wolff

A Sulzer RND 105 engine. These 'cathedral engines' produce 4000 h.p. per cylinder. Photo: Sulzer Bros Ltd

Three other features are certainly part of the changed scene. In terms of propulsion, fitting controllable pitch propellers, where the angle of the blades can be altered to suit differing operating conditions, has become widespread. Patents for controllable pitch propellers were taken out in the first part of the 19th century but it was not until recently that mechanical design and the standard of materials reached the stage where such propellers could be fitted and forgotten. Where ships have widely varying duties, perhaps sometimes deeply loaded and others lightly, near optimum propulsion can be achieved with this device which is particularly suitable for vessels which do a large part of their work at low speeds such as tugs, trawlers and the like.

Similarly, the propulsion duct, an airfoil section ring around a propeller, is now commonplace on many vessels which operate with highly loaded screws. Examples again are tugs, fishing vessels, bulk carriers and, indeed, VLCCs, where the use of such ducts is becoming increasingly common. With such a propulsion duct or nozzle, which produces thrust itself and improves propeller efficiency, a VLCC may attain an improvement in performance of around 15 per cent compared with the open propeller vessel and a tug may increase its tow rope pull by 30 or 40 per cent (page 57).

Finally, a great many vessels today fit bow thrusters –transversely mounted propellers or propulsion devices. Suitably controlled from the bridge, such thrusters, which again may be controllable pitch, greatly assist in berthing, in turning ferries off berths and in manoeuvring at low speeds generally. Indeed, the peak of such performance is reached with the dynamically positionable vessel where thrusters at bow and stern can be used to move the vessel in any direction. Drill rigs are an excellent example as are the latest cable ships which are capable of some 4 knots sideways and of being manoeuvred in any direction by means of a small joystick in the control station or by a computer.

All ships roll and a feature of the last 30 years has been the widespread acceptance of roll reduction devices. These are not new; a common type–an open tank across the ship approximately one third full of water–was first fitted in HMS *Inflexible* in the 1880s. The fin type, in effect a pair of horizontal rudders port and starboard, was first invented well before the Second World War and actually fitted in many British warships of that period. The other common type, the so-called closed U-tube tank, was fitted nearly 70 years ago, a notable installation being in the Cunard liner *Aquitania*.

However, the design of roll dampers is not easy

and it has taken the great growth of naval architectural science in the past 30 years to optimise design and performance. In essence, a ship rolls because the water level is higher on one side than the other. If levels vary at approximately the same rate as the ship will roll anyway in her natural period, then what is known as resonant rolling occurs and this can be violent. The essence of any stabilising system is to oppose the roll by a heeling moment in the opposite direction in antiphase to the wave moment. A great many ships of the ferry type, all passenger and cruise ships, many cargo liners, fishing vessels, cable ships, research ships and so on are now fitted with either tank or fin stabilisers or sometimes a combination of both.

Perhaps the most solid plank in the technological platform on which the era has been based is that provided by the digital computer. Not seen by the public and maybe even unsuspected, it plays today a dominant role in the design of ships and in the evolution of their new generations. It has also, curiously in this inflationary age, greatly reduced the cost of many design operations. For example, hydrostatics, the complicated graphs that describe how the ship's displacement, stability and trimming factors and so on change in relation to draft, were produced manually. Whether for a ship large or small this involved several man-weeks of time with corresponding cost. Today this is done on a computer in a matter of minutes at perhaps one tenth the cost. This is a simple example, but many of the larger and more complicated calculations connected with ships have been similarly simplified to even greater advantage. However, what is much more important really is the increased power that the digital computer has given to the naval architect and the effect it has had upon production. Many of the operations in a modern shipyard are performed by machines which are numerically controlled by tapes prepared for them

by a computer. Indeed, the machine has its own micro-computer to translate these tapes.

Much of the work of naval architecture is laborious and time-consuming if done manually. Whether it is weight and moment calculations or many of the calculations involving stability and strength, the output possible was, in the past, limited by the number of people available to do it. Indeed, some aspects of naval architecture were practically a closed book because of the immense human effort required to quantify usefully and practically the mathematical methods that were available. Calculation of the resistance produced by the waves made by a ship, detailed calculation of the local stresses in ship structures, the motions of ships in the extremely complex waves of a real sea, all posed problems of human capacity which, apart from occasional computation in research, were well nigh insoluble in production. The development of the digital computer has freed naval architects and shipbuilding from the slavery involved in many of its calculations and has made possible the direct computation of results which could only have been obtained in the past by analogue or model testing.

Ships are no longer drawn out in great detail. In the better equipped shipyards the shape of the ship is defined mathematically and the plating and sections are defined similarly. The hull shape is faired or 'made smooth' mathematically and instructions for the structural shops prepared in numerical form. However, the impact of the computer can go back much earlier to the formative stages when the optimum basic design of the ship is being settled. If a mathematical model of a ship's economics can be constructed in terms of basic parameters the effect of a great many variations in these can be explored rapidly to find the optimum basic design. The ship's behaviour can be explored in advance of construction or even model testing. Again, the solution of mathematical models of sea-keeping, motion response, loading and stress in waves, and of propulsion and manoeuvrability have all been made possible by the digital computer. This truly is a revolution. In 1950 even the possibility of what is now commonplace use of the computer would have been regarded as science fiction. It has, of course, produced change in naval architects themselves. Future generations will become more and more mathematical and inclined to explore possibilities of new and original ship types and propulsion systems.

The revolution has extended to operating ships. No longer can crews maintain vessels at sea. They are too few and the ships too large. Shore gangs and machinery do this work. No longer is navigation dependent on the sextant and the chronometer. Radar has transformed close quarters navigation while overall it has been equally affected by the development of radio methods such as Decca and Loran, by inertial navigation systems integrating the signals from gyroscopes and by the latterday development of satellite navigation using signals from navigational satellites. Most of these developments have their origins in the Second World War or subsequent weapons research development.

Painting systems and the protection of steel have improved immensely, and one of the most exciting developments of the 70s has been that of self-polishing polymers, coatings applied to underwater hull surfaces which do not get rougher with age but actually get smoother and inhibit the growth of organisms. A fuel saving of 12 per cent compared with more traditional paint and antifouling systems has been demonstrated on tankers. In a fuel hungry age, the considerable savings that modern paints and, in particular, selfpolishing polymers can produce are of the utmost significance.

Another influence for change is the emphasis today upon offshore work, whether the recovery of oil from offshore deposits or of seabed deposits from the deeps of minerals such as manganese nodules, metal rich muds, etc. The techniques needed for these activities have come from shipbuilding and have, in turn, spurred further development in it while other disciplines involved in these activities have fed many new ideas and approaches into shipbuilding itself.

It is an era of rapidly developing technology. If anything the pace today is accelerating. Herein lies the hope for the developed nations as it is a brutal fact of life that it is becoming increasingly difficult to build the simpler types of ships economically in such countries in competition with newly developed nations where the necessary capital has been invested in modern facilities and where labour is more cost effective. Just as, for example, in electronics, the hope of developed nations is in sophisticated new products requiring the wide variety of disciplinary skills, the comprehensive research and backup facilities and the capital that they possess, the same applies in shipping. Sophisticated services based on highly developed vessels and systems with as much automation as possible are the means for competition. The danger is always of standing still. Today it does not take long to reach a given level of engineering sophistication and the only safeguard is to move the level higher at least as fast as that.

This, then, is the so-called shipping revolution of the third quarter of the 20th century; an era of intense effort, great expansion in numbers, types and size of ships, but above all dominated by two factors, the integration of ships into overall transport systems and the willingness of all concerned to achieve anything provided it offered sound reasons, economic and technical, for so doing. It has been an exciting era for all concerned, whether shipowner, shipbuilder, naval architect or research worker, an era whose only peer is parts of the 19th century. Like them, it has been wearing but stimulating.

Propulsion ducts
around propellers
can much improve
their efficacy.
Photo: Mitsubishi Ltd and
Burness Corlett & Partners Ltd

Glossary

Block Coefficient	the ratio between the actual volume of the underwater body of a ship and that of the rectangular box that would contain it
Bo/Ro	Bulk/oil/Ro/ro
bow visor door	a section of bow that hinges up to allow vehicles to drive out
CBT	clean ballast tanks
cellular	vertical cells with guides for loading containers
COW	crude oil washing
cryogenic	extremely cold gases in liquid form
dunnage	packing between units of cargo
DWT	deadweight tonnage–the actual lifting capability of a ship
freeboard	the part of a hull above the waterline
GRT	gross registered tons–a measure of internal volume
hydrodynamics	the science of ship powering, propulsion and handling
IGS	inert gas systems
LASH	Lighter Aboard Ship
length between perpendiculars	length between the rudder stock and the load waterline forward
LNG	liquid natural gas (methane)
LPG	liquid petroleum gas (butane and propane)
LSD	Landing Ship Dock
OBO	oil/bulk/ore ship
Panamax	the largest size able to go through the Panama Canal
PCC	pure car carrier
PROBO	Product/oil/bulk/ore carrier
Ro/Ro	roll-on/roll-off
SBT	segregated ballast tanks
TEU	twenty equivalent units (equivalent to twenty foot containers)
ULCC	ultra large crude carrier
VLCC	very large crude carrier

Notes

[1] *Ships of the Invasion Fleet*, R.Baker, RINA Transactions, 1947.

[2] *Speed at Sea and Despatch in Port*, W.MacGillivray, RINA Transactions, 1948.

[3] *Speed at Sea and Despatch in Port* and *Cargo Access Equipment for Merchant Ships*, I.L.Buxton, C.P.Daggitt & J.King, McGregor Publications Ltd.

[4] *The Life of I.K.Brunel*, Isambard Brunel, Longmans Green 1870.

[5] *Ships Cargo–Cargo Ships*, eds. H.Kummerman and R.Jacquinet, MacGregor Publications 1979.

[6] *Ships of the Invasion Fleet*.

Index

THE SHIP

The complete list of titles in this major series of ten books on the development of the ship is as follows:

1. *Rafts, Boats and Ships From Prehistoric Times to the Medieval Era* Sean McGrail
2. *Long Ships and Round Ships Warfare and Trade in the Mediterranean 3000 BC–500 AD* John Morrison
3. *Tiller and Whipstaff The Development of the Sailing Ship : 1400–1700* Alan McGowan
4. *The Century before Steam The Development of the Sailing Ship : 1700–1820* Alan McGowan
5. *Steam Tramps and Cargo Liners : 1850–1950* Robin Craig
6. *Channel Packets and Ocean Liners : 1850–1970* John M. Maber
7. *The Life and Death of the Merchant Sailing Ship : 1815–1965* Basil Greenhill
8. *Steam, Steel and Torpedoes The Warship in the 19th Century* David Lyon
9. *Dreadnought to Nuclear Submarine* Antony Preston
10. *The Revolution in Merchant Shipping : 1950–1980* Ewan Corlett

All titles in *The Ship* series are available from:
HER MAJESTY'S STATIONERY OFFICE

Government Bookshops

49 High Holborn, London WC1V 6HB
13a Castle Street, Edinburgh EH2 3AR
41 The Hayes, Cardiff CF1 1JW
Brazennose Street, Manchester M60 8AS
Southey House, Wine Street, Bristol BS1 2BQ
258 Broad Street, Birmingham B1 2HE
80 Chichester Street, Belfast BT1 4JY

Government publications are also available through booksellers

The full range of Museum publications is displayed and sold at
National Maritime Museum
Greenwich

HMSO BOOKS

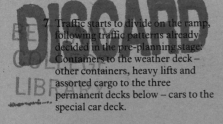

7 Traffic starts to divide on the ramp, following traffic patterns already decided in the pre-planning stage: Containers to the weather deck – other containers, heavy lifts and assorted cargo to the three permanent decks below – cars to the special car deck.

8 All internal ramps have expanded steel deck surfaces, a 1:8 gradient and a long radius transition from rise to flat. This maximizes speed of handling. The hydraulically operated ramp covers become part of the deck when lowered.

9 Cargo on all decks is handled mechanically the ship's own equipment, which includes 6 large fork lift trucks, 1 heavy duty tug mast top- and side-handling equipment etc. Load and unloading can take place simultaneous Supervisors and ship's personnel drive rou on 'golf carts' keeping walkie-talkie contact with each other and with the office contain Cargo is finally secured by a special system ties which hold it safely in place.

6 The quarter ramp is designed to allow loading/unloading at any port with standard quays and tidal variations of up to 33'. The ramp has a load bearing capacity of up to 400 tons. It is 39'6" wide and takes two lines of traffic, loading or unloading up to 800 tons per hour. This reduces time spent in port and so cuts down total transit times.

5 All loading and unloading operations are controlled by a Barber Blue Sea loading specialist, working from an office container which is carried as part of the ship's equipment and is parked at the stern ramp while the ship is in port. This control is a key point in the BBS SuperCarrier system.

4 Self-powered cargo drives straight on board just as it is, either from the road, from its transport vehicle or from the marshalling yards. Low loaders with heavy cargo are towed on board by tug masters. This means that there is no demounting or remounting – no damage from lifting.

3 20' containers are either driven on board singly by top- or side-handling fork lift trucks, or loaded two together onto 40' slave trailers. 40' containers are also loaded onto 40' slave trailers. Loaded slave trailers are towed on board by tug masters (hustlers).

2 Cargo which is not containerized by the shipper is offloaded direct into the stuffing shed – sorted – tallied – and stuffed into containers, bin containers or onto flats. Bin containers and flats are stored under cover, containers are taken straight on board or stacked in the container yard.